ÜNAL ÇOBAN

THE CODE
OF DESTINY

DESTEK
yayınları

DESTEK PUBLISHING: 1656
SELF-IMPROVEMENT: 287

ÜNAL GÜNER / THE CODE OF DESTINY

Privilege Owner: Destek Yapım Prodüksiyon Dış Tic. A.Ş.
Editor in Chief: Ertürk Akşun
Publications Coordinator: Özlem Esmergül
Production Coordinator: Semran Karaçayır
Translated by Ebru Gündem
Edited by Don Dungan Jr.
Cover Design by Ilknur Muştu
Page Design by Cansu Poroy
Social Media – Graphic Design by Tuğçe Budak-Mesud Topal-Meltem Kökboyun

Destek Publishing: October 2022
Certificate# 13226

ISBN 978-625-441-775-7

© Destek Yayınları
Abdi İpekçi Caddesi No. 31/5 Nişantaşı/İstanbul
Tel. (0) 212 252 22 42
Fax: (0) 212 252 22 43
www.destekyayinlari.com
info@destekyayinlari.com
facebook.com/ DestekYayinevi
twitter.com/destekyayinlari
instagram.com/destekyayinlari.com

Printed at Deniz Ofset Deniz Ofset – Çetin Koçak
Sertifika No. 48625
Maltepe Mahallesi
Hastane Yolu Sokak No. 1/6
Zeytinburnu / İstanbul
Tel. (0) 212 613 30 06

Destek Dukkan

ÜNAL GÜNER

THE CODE OF DESTINY

Secret (musical) notes within words, events and situations

CATCH THE RHYTHM OF LIFE

Translated by
Ebru Gündem

Edited by
Don Dungan Jr.

DESTEK
yayınları

CONTENTS

PART V: READING LIFE BY EXAMINING THE BODY

PART VI: READING THE POSITIVE AND NEGATIVE

As we begin...

Ever since the day I discovered that the flow of life and most importantly destiny have mathematics, and that this mathematics has a secret language, I have been trying to decode it. I imagine myself as the director of a movie, of which I am the screenwriter, editor and casting director. I strive to understand, within my plot, the place of everything and everyone entering the frame of my camera. Sometimes, I also get the feeling that something is off. In such cases, I ask myself: "Why might this actor have been involved in my story; why might I have invited events to which I would object?"

Although I do not find and figure out the answers right away, I reconsider what has happened and what it has told me.

Things that occur in front of me, the health of my body, the dreams that I have, my expressions and what I feel as a result of all these are in constant conversation with me. In fact, what truly matters is the conversation. Life seems like a foreign language at times... You hear it, listen to it, watch it and speak with it... Yet, you may have difficulty understanding it. If you simply label it as "destiny" and move on, time will pass but events and how they make you feel will linger.

Destiny is the value you assign to your own life.

The geography you were born into has a rhythm, a flavor and a scent that permeates on you. There might be unchangeable codes of the reality you were born into: you might have been raised somewhere far from school; you might have lost a parent; you might have had financial strains. It does not mean that you will not reach financial abundance or that you will not become a good parent.

Surely, what has brought you to where you have not been your free choices, but the best ones among the choices you were presented with. You may call this "My Invariable Destiny!" However, destiny has variable parameters, as well. The process starting with birth has impacts on the future. Nevertheless, it is up to you whether or not this process will encompass your whole future. This is exactly where the destiny software may be updated.

Only you know your own value. There are things you accept, and things you do not accept in the face of events. What makes you choose something; how do you determine your choices? Could you make your own choices, unleashing yourself from the family in which you grew up, from your surroundings, your culture, or your rote knowledge? Naturally, the projection of the past would reflect your choices whether you realize it or not. This might keep going up to the point where the cover of your past spread on you is elevated. Of course, you cannot fully change the factors that have brought you into existence, yet you can change your perspective on the connection you have with these factors. When you are freed from the cover of the "past," you become the ruler of your own life and you are sure of your decisions. You are the one holding the responsibility for your life and choices, and you can renew them whenever you like. If you are not sure when you make your decisions, you may object to the results of the events, and feel hindered.

What determines whether a person regrets or is sure of their decisions is whether or not they are in their center while they are making these decisions.

What does being in your center mean?

It is to grasp the rhythm of life and to be able to go forward with it. It is to be able to take heed of the inspirations of the future through the guidance of the knowledge attained from the roots. It is to approach the new courageously, and to bring knowledge and action together.

You might be asking: "What takes you away from your own center?"

My answer would be: "Holding on tightly to what you already know, wanting to stay in your comfort zone, and resisting change." As time goes forward, regression would start once you say, "Let me stop for a while." The repetitive cycle of the past is activated precisely at this point. The belief that you will experience the same creates the perception that destiny will not change. You can see destiny as software loaded onto your computer by your potential.

In this book, I share the language of the software that I have just mentioned. This language will help you to make sense of the things you experience. You will notice that everything that happens has a cause; and that each of those you disregard as a coincidence is a sign. As you learn the secret language of life, you may update your own life's software. You may reconsider your choices and renew the behavior patterns in which you are stuck. Since everything that reflects from you defines you, the results of even a miniscule change will reflect upon you as major transformations. Sometimes, a word changes and the events you go through, your feelings and even your dreams will undergo a change. When the posture of your body changes, an organ will heal; when you smile, the conflicts that you are experiencing with someone will turn into harmony.

Behind your choices is your potential, and behind your potential is a perfect mathematical system... Now, we start an enjoyable ride with this book. Let us read together the secret language of life.

About the Author

Ünal Güner was born in 1966, in Gaziantep, Turkey, as the only child of a family whose roots trace back to Caucasus on one side and to Egypt on the other. When he was in the third grade of Çapa Primary School, he was enrolled in a judo class by his father who was a former wrestler. In this period, he was trained in judo, aikido and jujutsu by internationally renowned masters who came to Turkey from Japan, Germany and England. He was on the Turkish national judo team for many years, which provided him the opportunity to represent Turkey as well as to get to know different cultures. In time, he started to work on the path to transfer physical power and abilities into emotion and soul.

After graduating from Şehremini High School, he started studying Physical Education and Sports at Marmara University. While still a student, he started teaching judo at the Turkish Naval Academy. Meanwhile, he combined learning with breathing techniques and worked at language education centers on learning through relaxation, focusing and sophrology systems. In 1988, he gave seminars and courses in the area of metaphysics. In 1989, he worked as the Health Director at Turkey's first health and detox hotel. While giving therapy lessons to physiotherapists about body therapy, and magnetism and manual therapy to trainers in different fields of sports, he also conducted breathing and hypnotherapy sessions for people and groups from many different fields.

In 1991, he completed his master's degree from the Faculty of Health Sciences at Marmara University. He wrote his thesis on "Sports Physiology and Psychology." Meanwhile, he gave courses on war, physical education and judo at the Turkish Air Force Academy. He has worked in a variety of fields, including reflexology, shiatsu, hypnotherapy, kinesiology, breathing training, tachyon, sound and color therapies. He continues to give courses in these areas.

instagram.com/unalguner

Facebook.com /unalguner

youtube.com/unalguner

bilgi@unalguner.com

www.unalguner.com

I wholeheartedly thank to
Yelda Cumalıoğlu who opened the path
for the book;
to Özlem Esmergül, my editor who applied
the information in my book on herself and to whom
I entrusted my work to with a peace of mind....

What Language Does Life Speak?

You actually feel how your day will turn out in the morning while you are preparing to start the day. The day has a flavor, a flow, a blockage, an openness, health, rhythm and a sense. It even has a destiny. You may even think that all this consciousness was transmitted to you through a dream. This state is also reflected in your statements from the moment you wake up. You have a demand from the day. You want to greet yourself first and then those around you. Some mornings, for instance, you wake up reticent and you want the day to never start.

Well, what do you think might be the reason for this?

An influence, an energy, the rhythm of life, your experiences...

Whichever it might be, they all follow one another. Life has an unheard, even unknown language, and this language speaks to you at any given moment. The encounters, reunions and the closing of the day are indicated through the feeling you wake up with...

It is just the same as how you know, or you feel like you know someone at first sight although you have not spoken with them yet. When you look into the eyes of a stranger, you sense right away whether they are peaceful, affectionate, grumpy or agreeable. It all surfaces in those few seconds. You are kind of affected by the other person.

Even though you begin to ignore certain things about that person, life will eventually prove how accurate your feelings were in those first few seconds.

Events, too, have a state of being, a starting point and a maturation. As you are signing up for a partnership that will end as of the moment it begins, is it destiny that commands the hand holding the pen? As you lend your phone charger that you know you will not receive back, is it forgotten to be returned each time because you said, "Don't forget to give it back!", or do you remind them to return it because you sense that the person will forget it in the first place? Do you believe that the effects occurring in your body following a troublesome event have something to do with you saying, "You'll make me ill"? In what language does life speak to us, does this language have a name? When do we need this language?

Just as talking is only one means to communicate, along with our feelings, body language and our gazes; many elements come together when we communicate with life. The utterances we use when expressing a request, our evaluations of events, our interpretation of dreams, our bonds with our emotions, our approach to our body, our communication with all other living beings, and even life itself... they are all intertwined and interconnected. When you grasp what is happening in one of these, you also understand the other. The language I am referring to reveals that thing also has a reality beyond what is visible. The orientation toward the call of reality is ignited by the curiosity as to how life works, and by the love you feel inside.

There is a system, a mathematics and an alphabet to meet reality. You can learn them, satisfy your curiosity, and open your eyes. Our endeavor to understand and make sense of life takes us away from lingering, inner unrest, and the crowd of the outside into the homeliness of the inner self. Once you accept and appreciate the gift of life presented to you, you also read the note from the one that gave you the gift. You can even read on that note about your future, about the messages of your body, your needs, about how you have come to the present moment, what is left of your relationships, what you did, what you could not do, about your obstacles, the holes and the bumps in front of you, and the purpose of your coming to this life.

Just as the first verse of the Qur'an starts with "Read" and has such reminders as 'Don't you read what is spread in front of your eyes,' the center of many religions and philosophies is right at this point. The invitation to unity is to stop separating, to receive the message of what happens, to be enlightened by enlightening your own way with a conceding heart. Contemplation and meditation are, therefore, recommended so that **one** would look inside and listen to **himself/herself.** The mind, which only calms when it is withdrawn, starts to watch and sees much more clearly beyond the visible.

You, too, will experience this clear vision once you begin to read life in the language it speaks. The first prerequisite to reach this point is to free yourself from judgments and be able to come to your center. What will keep you at your center is to get rid of the act of defining yourself through others through the realization that you let others decide who you are, and take this authority from them. This way, you abandon the effort of having their approval and persuading them, and move on to appreciate your own value. When you navigate from the inside to the outside, you become the one holding the reins of the bonds to the outside.

When we are at our center, we begin to 'witness.' There is no aspect to watching, no limitation to the look, and no interpretation of the event. Otherwise, we will no longer be witness, but a party to the event, whereas life's invitation to us is to be a witness. Only then, the balance of the scale is set and we find peace. Trying to be good or attempting to be bad would disrupt the balance of the scale.

Years ago, I used to regard being good as superior. The idea that "people are quintessentially good, so they must be telling the truth" prevented me from understanding who is doing what and why. I was biased towards what was happening around me. Presuming that what people said was actually what they meant, I would fail to receive the message shining beyond what was seen, and I would turn out to be wrong. So, I asked myself, "What should I do?" OK, they might be wrong, incomplete, or on the side of the darkness right now, but maybe they could get on the side of the light if they are helped. Then I tried to save them in my own way.

This approach shows that I still had a judgmental view to life, but I only realized it much later. I did not trust the system, thinking "Solely under my control, if I do, if I intervene," and acting accordingly. I was trying to correct using my own interpretation of the events and people I described as bad and dark. This act disturbed both me and my reflections, but I was still ignoring it. Many of the events I attempted to control and manage were getting out of hand and always ended up opposite of what I was trying to do. My effort to save people and the world, as it turned out, was actually my effort to free myself from this situation. I was wasting the labor I would put on myself, and the resources I would use for my maturation. As I was trying to lead them to my path, they were coming to show me that I was moving away from my own center. This was the reason for the inner disputes between us; clearly, you could not change someone's path by forcing them; you could illuminate the path of those who seek the light and are willing to start their journey only when you illuminate your own light.

When you start reading what is beyond the visible, all you need to remember is that what you call 'outside' does actually exist to tell you about yourself.

"Focus on your own center,
without turning into darkness, without worshipping the light."

Although a jellyfish consists of ninety-nine percent water, it has a boundary by which it can separate itself from water... Whereas I was lost as to where my own boundary ended and that of the sea began. What I had learned up to that point was that all of us were the sea. I did not know what boundary meant. It was wrong for me to draw lines and not give what you have. It felt more right to give until you run out of what you have in your pocket and give support until you run out of energy. "If we were not to trust people and life, if we were not to rush toward each other's call for help, how would we describe being human?" I was asking myself. I became a good person in my own right by not saying no, actually by not being able to say no. This state of presumption was my weakness for a long time. In order to find my direction, I decided to focus and listen, and stay in the state of watching. I started reading events, realizing first the subtexts and then the things that I had ignored by hiding them from the outside and myself. I started to gradually notice that what seems to happen and what actually does are totally different. Over time, I figured that the subconscious mind, the body and nature have a common mathematical language. My initial weakness later helped me become stronger in this area.

Koichi Tohei, whose physical movements were restricted, especially because his lungs were inadequate due to pleurisy he had suffered as a child, transformed his weakness into such a strength that he became one of the leading aikido masters in the world by substituting the physical energy that he felt lacking in himself with 'chi' energy. He augmented the chi energy in his body so much that, with his magnetic field, he could neutralize dozens of people who were simultaneously attacking him.

In fact, the weakness or deficiency of each one of us in a certain area is for us to work on and transfer our strength into that area. The disciples, who are trained in the Far Eastern martial arts from childhood on, hit objects with their hands so swiftly that their bones are broken. Once the healing process of the bone is over, it becomes stronger than before. The disciples are asked to repeat this movement over and over, until their bones become strong as steel because the body piles up more bone tissue in that area to repair the missing and weak section after each fracture.

As I learned to read life through words, events, and situations, I grasped the significance of knowing how to use the powers we possess. Reading life does not only bring you to your own center, but it also frees you from drawing on other people's approval. Reading what has happened takes you away from time shifts about the past, and reading what will happen takes you away from time shifts about the future, thus leading you to living in the present. This way, you can move on to live in peace and acceptance.

> *"Reading what happens illuminates the past,*
> *and reading what will happen illuminates the future. "*

The knowledge of reading what has happened over thousands of years is being used technically today thanks to developing technology, artificial intelligence, in other words, thanks to machines. A great deal of physical and energy information about a human being can be analyzed instantly through a sample taken from them. While we believe in the detection and diagnosis of the machines that we design with the knowledge we transfer from ourselves, we sometimes cannot benefit from this wisdom that we own. We do not believe we possess this wisdom. Wisdom is to use knowledge in the right place.

My effort to understand the human and what is happening, along with my interest in technological developments also helped me feed on scientific studies in my endeavor. The frequency measurement devices that I use, too, in my studies can display a person's DNA analysis, the current state inside a cell, genetic potentials, the flow of energy centers in the body, aura photographing, as well as the person's emotional, mental and psychological state. Thanks to the application of the physiognomy literature containing reading techniques of the eye, tongue, teeth and face, very deep analyses of these can be made. However, I would like to remind you that each of us has the capacity and power to reach data far beyond the diagnostics made by machines and computers.

We can make sense of ourselves and our experiences with these methods, providing us with possibly an infinite number of reading options. I aimed to make the subject more understandable and applicable by combining the reading techniques in the book with my own experiences and realizations.

I spent my childhood in the triangle of Malatya, Gaziantep and Istanbul. Winters in Istanbul, in summers first in my mother's hometown Gaziantep, and then my father's hometown Malatya Doğanşehir... I have some sayings in my life that I fell in love with, of which I heard before even learning how to read and write, before even knowing their meanings. Two such sayings are: "Whatever is in the world, is in the man" and "Knowledge was just one point, the ignorant multiplied it"...

Later in life, as I learned the meanings of these sayings, my admiration grew even deeper. The multitude was emerging from a single point. When I could learn to know one thing thoroughly, I could have an idea about many things. I asked myself: "Well, Ünal, would it be possible to read the WHOLE if you can focus on yourself -that is a man, a human being- and on ONE single point of yourself?"

The answer is in this book ...

Naturally, it is possible to read the WHOLE by looking at the ONE...

Because all parts belong to the whole.

The way a cell divides and forms our body from nearly thirty trillion cells is the same as a seed turning into hundreds of fruit-bearing trees. Those who can read life meet themselves and rejoin their essence.

PART I

READING LIFE

Secret Alphabet Inside Words, Events and Situations

Life is a very valuable book that has been given to us as a present... When we do not know the language and alphabet of this book, we naturally cannot read it. When we cannot read it, we may become angry, offended and furious. We may even question the giver of this present, saying, "Why did you give me this present which I do not know the meaning of? How am I going to deal with all these events that make me so sad, angry, upset, that hurt me from time to time, that seem unfair sometimes, of which I cannot solve the math, and that I mostly cannot control?" We often hold the giver responsible for many undesirable events that happen to us.

We project anger and blame first on others and then on the 'proprietor of the system.' However, when we learn the alphabet of life and begin to read what happens, we begin to spell out the causes of our experiences. All of a sudden, we notice that the book of life tells us many things of which we are not aware at all; that, in fact, every event flows exactly as it should, in a wonderful system of harmony and mathematics. When we flow with it, we hear its rhythm; and when we resist it, we lose time and get tired.

Of course, the system expects labor from our side in order to learn how to read life. If you are willing to be a reader, this book is ready to guide you.

Basically, there are two ways to read people and life.

1. **Reading from inside:** It is reading through the heart's eye by unveiling the heart. The journey to opening the veil on the heart's eye begins with attaining the meaning, by noticing and watching from your own center the reflection of what is outside in you. Your heart is where all the knowledge of what has happened and will be happening is stored.

2. **Reading from outside:** It is reading what you watch, hear and experience outside. It is reading the events reflected in the mirror of life, as well as your expressions, emotions, social relationships, family, and body. This sets in motion the journey to your own center.

If we are going to read from the mirror of life, we naturally stand in front of the mirror and think that what we are watching is the "outside". When we want to change a situation, our first move is towards the reflection from the mirror. We assume that when we change it, we will change life. We may pour our energy, our focus until their last drop. However, no matter what we do, what is watched does not change. What changes is the approach and perspective towards what is being watched.

***

How will we change the world, how will we save it?

We cannot change the world; we can contribute to it through our contribution to life. We cannot save the world, but we can save ourselves from ignorance.

How do we shape others the way we want?

We cannot shape anyone; we cannot make someone evolve. We can only guide those who ask for help.

In a Zen monastery, when the master was asked by his disciple as to how he could save the world, the master's answer was precise: "Go and wash the dishes."

Transformation starts with you...

When you take and put aside a stone on your way, you open not only your own path, but also the path of those who will come after you. If you act with the sentiment of saving others while lifting this stone, you will be underestimating the organizing power of life, and putting yourself in the place of the savior, thus ignoring your own worth and journey. When you realize that you are serving the entirety while lifting that stone to clear your way, you will remember that you are a part of that entirety. You will be listening to the voice of your heart whispering to you the desire to lift that stone from the ground. At that moment, the savior and the saved are one. If you lift the stone not for yourself but to save someone else, the part of you thinking that you will not hear the voice of your heart may cause you to be arrogant. You will have separated it from yourself, and yourself from the system. We are all part of the whole.

When you look in the mirror to see yourself, to get rid of the acne on your face, you naturally squeeze the acne on your face; you do not reach for the image in the mirror. The function of the mirror is to reflect what is in you.

So is the mirror of life. What is in front of you makes you realize what is in you. You may either try to change it and get exhausted in vain, or return to yourself and get rid of it.

So is the process of understanding and learning life. All spiritual studies, teachings, those who guide the effort to enlightenment and understanding life will tell us to turn inward, and look in ourselves for whatever we are looking for.

What you object to, what you cannot accept are the ones
you cannot make sense of.
When you understand why; when you accept that what has
happened to you is neither a punishment nor a reward, and that it
is only 'what has happened; life flows and the way opens up.
The world is the point of conceiving the unity
of the watcher and the watched.

Look at Yourself in the Mirror

If it is yourself who you are watching in the mirror,
can you be exempted from what you object to?

"What is life?" You may have given different answers to
this question at different times: "What is life for you?"

Now answer this question once more...
To me, ...
life is work.

life is fun.

life is family.

life is an occupation.

life is rhythm.

life is difficult.

life is discovery.

life is responsibility. life is sharing.

life is accepting.

life is valuing.

life is joy.

life is music.

life is a fight.

The answer you give actually defines h...
life until now, what you have done and wha... lived you...
have come here for. This does not mean that...tiny you
in the same way. You can make a new defini...continue
perspective.   ...a new

**Those who leave the past in yesterday can be bor...
into a new future tomorrow.**

I had an uncle, Mehmet, who retired from the railways. "L...e
is work," he used to say. For this reason, he devoted himse...
to working to earn money until his last breath. As a man who
reached an old age, his will was to donate his body as a cadaver
to medical school students. Even after he died, his lifeless body
continued to work as a teacher.

Another acquaintance of mine used to say that life was
all about troubles and difficulties. What kind of life do you
think he lived? Of course, he lived pretending to escape from
these difficulties in appearance while attracting what he
escaped from into his life. As the phrase goes, "the weed he
disliked naturally ended up right under his nose." If you *are*
complaining about something, that is, if you are objecting to
it, you are inviting them into your life. This acquaintance I
mentioned used to constantly complain about the problems he
encountered. One day, I couldn't stop myself from asking him:
"Is it possible that you want to make your life more difficult
by constantly using the word difficult and complaining about
life?"

"Am I crazy?" he snapped. "Does anyone ever want to
complicate their own life?"

I kept quiet. He didn't realize that what came out of his
mouth would be put in front of him like an order he placed at a

...e been aware, he would not have been ordering restau...ay. To him, the culprit was on the outside.

diffic...ice, another friend of mine with whom everything ...used to say "It'll work out." As you can imagine, goe...g worked out somehow.

eve...k of life as the four walls of a room. One of the walls is ...one is states and predicaments, another is expressions, ...e last one is dreams. These four elements constitute the structure and the whole of life. The awareness experienced in ...one of them affects the whole room, and life is transformed. For example, the experiences you draw into your life by saying "Absolutely" are not limited to events, but this habit can also set the groundwork for various ailments in the body. People who use the word "absolutely" often have ailments in their gall bladder, liver, knee or neck. When the state that causes this expression changes, that is, when the person yields and starts to say "Maybe," things begin to soften and the body starts to recover. This is also reflected in dreams and tension turns into relaxation.

Words are the source of events, events are the source of feelings, and feelings are the source of dreams. In the cycle of life, each factor creates the other. Once you realize the destiny you have called for in one of them, change and awakening begin in the others.

The system has a very simple mechanism. The moment you realize this, you will witness that many areas in your life change easily. All of this happens when you realize your connection with life and turn towards yourself.

Those who want to change their world witness miracles as they transform themselves.

Factors That Form Life

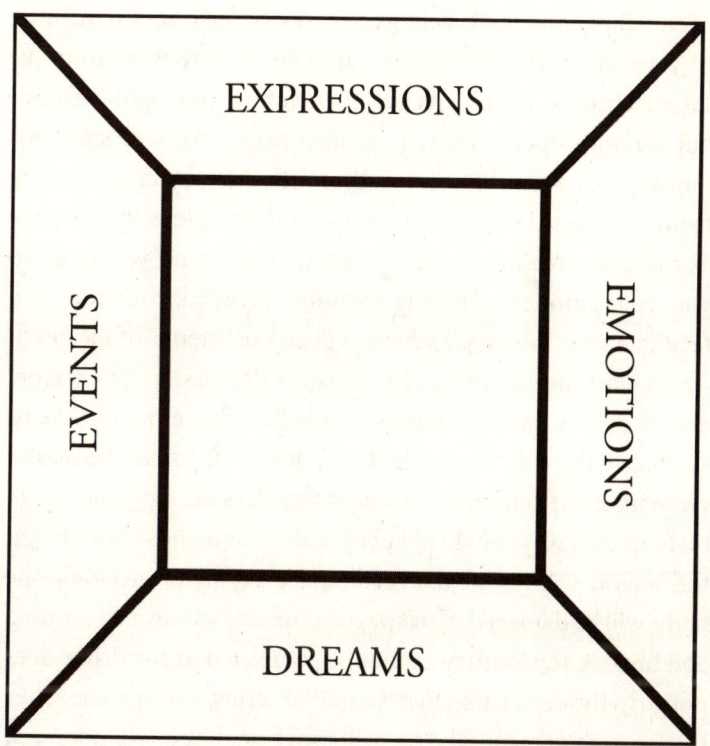

In the cycle of destiny, each factor creates another. Those who wake up in just one wake up in all of them. Those who can make changes even in one of them experience changes in all.

Thus, life also changes. You, too, will be transformed.

You, too, can invite the rain of miracles into your life. You can pay attention to your expressions, follow the flow of events, realize the state you are in, and benefit from the guidance of dreams. Maybe your mind may try to object to what I have been telling you, your feelings may resist, the traces remaining in your memories from your experiences may want to prove their rightness. In the journey of evolution, not righteousness, but serenity opens the veil of one's heart. We will start this journey that we will go on together with the subject of "reading from the outside". Afterwards, we will complete the journey as the ones "reading from the heart." Your mind will listen to you, your emotions will help you move forward, your body will facilitate your journey, and you will be the listener of the heart.

To illustrate; let's think of a carriage with horses, reins, wagon, driver and a master: horses symbolize the emotions, reins symbolize the will, wagon the body, driver the mind, the master symbolizes the soul, and the road symbolizes life. If the horses go on their own way and do not obey to the commands of the driver, the wagon will go off the road, and everything, including the body, will be damaged. If the wagon is unable to move on the road and broken, the journey cannot be completed. If the driver does not go to the destination that the master wants, if he does not obey the master's demand, the car will move on, but it will not reach the destination. Without the reins, the driver cannot handle the horses. Here, the journey is complete when the carriage, horses, and the driver serve the master together as a means to reach the destination, otherwise the journey turns into a loss.

In the soul's journey, in order for the evolution to take place, the mind must apply the commands it receives through the will and be able to manage the emotions, and the body must serve this progress.

Every expression, emotion and action belong to their owner. They all work like a boomerang and return to their owner. This is the mechanism that has been meant for thousands of years by the saying "You reap what you sow!"

The Common Alphabet of Life

Writings, numbers and our spoken language...

Each of these is for communication through symbols.

Alright, but does the universe have another language?

Computers basically do billions of operations with the sequence of two symbols: Zero and One... These numbers come in front of and behind each other, forming a matrix. With two such simple symbols, all those operations work perfectly. 'YES' and 'NO' are marked in the coordinates of the mechanism that answers almost all of our questions. We come across this two-optioned language of life over and over as give-take, income-expenditure, masculine-feminine, past-future, approval-rejection, right-left.

What should come, what should stay, what should go?

The mood of hesitation freezes like a computer infected with a virus and may destroy the information it seeks.

Think about the moments when you cannot decide, you are in hell during those moments.

Decision making mechanism helps you choose between being yourself and being you of whom others approve.

For example, "What are your expectations from a relationship?" It is easy to answer this question. However, what really matters is being able to evaluate whether or not to have a relationship with someone who does not meet your expectations. You have 'yes' and 'no' in your decision-making mechanism, how you use them makes you free or captive.

In this relationship, my expectations of attention, loyalty, sharing, trust... are met.

I expect enthusiasm, happiness, joy… from this relationship. My relationship lacks the properties of courtesy, understanding, caring… I distress over economic concerns, insecurity, and not being valued in this relationship.

I love very much the enthusiasm, high energy, respect, honesty… in this relationship.

I fear that there will be separation, abandonment, infidelity, attachment to the past, habits, or disconnections due to workaholism in this relationship.

I want this relationship to be full of affection, love, pleasure and taste…

I am not happy with the arguments, the lack of time, the lack of understanding, the insults, the loud talking… in this relationship.

In this relationship, my expectations of respect, value, loyalty… are not met.

I see this relationship as a waste of time.

I exist in this relationship.

I do not exist in this relationship.

I have a financial expectation from this relationship.

I have an emotional expectation from this relationship.

I am hopeful about the future of this relationship.

This relationship has no future.

I can never accept the behavior of violence, insults, disrespect, infidelity, irresponsibility… in this relationship.

It is crucial for you to be able to ask yourself questions in order to clearly identify the current situation of your relationships and to see clearly what to do next.

Like logarithms in computers, we, too, can evaluate many parameters by listing them one under the other and make our choices.

In other words, we can make our choices by having 1 and 0 in front of us. When you do the listing above, you can easily make your decision about whether to continue the relationship and can predict the results of your choices.

All decisions are made this way. 'Yes' and 'No' will help you move forward. In the matter of where to go and not, you determine your course, just as the reins control the horses in the example of the carriage. For the yes-no system to work properly, your ego must have established your area like a circle. Ego is the area where you define yourself and connect with your environment. Here the stage is yours. The emergence of your existence is secured thanks to this circle. If your circle is uncertain, you will hesitate to implement your decisions and the system will collapse.

While teaching children their own limits, we first put our hand on our own chest and say "Me". Then we rest our hand on their chest and say "you." Thus, we teach the child to protect their own space and not to harm others. While fulfilling their wishes, we set the limits with yes and no commands.

For example, "Yes, you can have that toy." "No, you can't eat that pizza." "Yeah, we can go to the park," etc.

This is also how we program what we desire. "Yes, I will continue my life like this." "No, I will not end this relationship."

Another name for the "Yes-No" coding principle is positive and negative.

Positive: Start – move forward – continue – rise – fill – move, etc...

Negative: End –stay put – reduce – lower – empty –stagnate, etc...

When we say "Life is one", the two poles of the "one" are formed at that moment. We can call it whether positive or negative, or matter-antimatter, or night-day. As can be seen in the table below, the scarcity, abundance or balance of masculine and feminine principles determine the shape and course of events in your life.

MASCULINE	FEMININE
Father	Mother
Male	Female
Future	Past
Son	Daughter
To give	To receive
Soul	Body
Above	Below
Hot	Cold
Fire	Water
Positive	Negative
Sun	Moon
Vertical	Horizontal
Fullness	Emptiness
Sky	Ground
Yang	Yin
Hard	Soft
Expenditure	Income
Concern	Fear
Lightness	Darkness
Bathroom	Kitchen
Right	Left
Front	Back
Top	Bottom
External	Internal
Dynamic	Lethargic
Day	Night

You can use this dual reading language of life in every event you experience. Just like the 0-1 coding system in computer programming, you can read life in the masculine and the feminine coding system, thus create solutions with the principles and the mathematics of this coding system.

In order to be able to read beyond the visible and decipher the codes of life, you must meticulously put these principles in place like the pieces of a puzzle.

It is important that the computer codes are in the right places in order to be able to read them correctly. Do your experiences stem from the repetition of patterns you learned in the past or do they contain messages about the future? This is where you must focus like an oracle to reveal the secrets. You should be able to read the signals of a disease by noticing what is going on in your body before that disease occurs. This is how you can realize the energy leaks, imbalance of emotions and thoughts, thus come back to your center by repairing yourself.

The universe reads every particle according to its vibrational speed and wavelengths. All objects and atoms have a vibration and sound in the environment they belong to. The same principle applies to light. The light that comes to our world from the sun is white. It undergoes atmospheric refraction, so we perceive it as yellow. We perceive the sky and water as blue. What enables us to perceive the seven colors of the rainbow is the differing of light in wavelengths after its diffraction when it hits clouds and water droplets.

This principle works similarly in our body. Each organ has its own vibration and sound wave. If you think of your body as an orchestra and your organs as instruments, the melody emanating from that orchestra is the trace you leave to the universe. This rhythm can be disrupted in a physical, mental or emotional discomfort that occurs in you.

The echo of the sound that each particle emits by vibrating reaches the entire universe and is not lost. For this reason, we can presume that sound initiates the first movement and carries the energy that provides its existence in every action.

That's why, it is important to start with 'EXPRESSION' while reading life.

Read! What is reflected from you to life,
from life to you...

Reading From Expression

Every action, verbal or non-verbal, carries an expression unique to its owner. In other words, the tone of your voice, the words you choose while speaking, your posture, your facial expressions, your gestures, your look, your smile, your laughter are the elements that define you.

You may think that you are acting only with your mind in your choices. However, the real choices spread with the music of your body. The mind determines, the language serves, but the old emotions trapped inside, disturbed body frequencies do not support your effort to improve your life. It is as if you suddenly stumble and you drop the novelty tray you are carefully carrying on the floor.

You want to learn and apply some knowledge with the intention to improve your life, but you cannot take action. You know that going for a walk in the morning will be good for you, so you decide to do so while going to bed in the evening, but you may not be able to implement this decision in the morning. In order to be able to change your choices, you need to notice what you cannot change. If you take the decision you make at night by convincing yourself through your mind, you cannot implement that decision in the morning. Persuasion is like listening to good music at a concert, it is good for you at the moment, but the effect starts to fade away after the concert. Improving the rhythm of the body-mind-emotion orchestra by realizing what is in you will also improve your life, and your choices will fall into place. You will stop persuading yourself to walk in the morning and as soon as you get up you will prepare for a walk.

To improve your choices, you have to be aware of your choices. You can do this through deep listening.

So, what is deep listening?

First, you will begin to hear yourself, what comes out of your mouth, what spreads from your body, and decipher your codes. You should watch your frequently repeated verbal expressions, facial expressions, walking, sitting, getting up, lying down, which will contribute to your awakening. Your emotions, thoughts and states that are stuck can give direction to your current voice and words, and this is reflected in the rhythm of your internal organs.

With your every move, you display an expression which is unique to you. This expression of yours is your definition in the universe. Just like your name, the vibrational range and speed of your expressions also have a mathematical measure.

Think of expressions where the word is the same but the frequency is different. For example, "Excuse me?"

The result it creates is different when you say it with a vibration of anger and when you say it with a vibration of love.

Even though the word is seemingly the same, the frequency that is loaded into the word changes the result. The frequency you are calling determines your order and its delivery method.

The action initiated by vibrations corresponds to a number and a digit in the universe.

Life began with a sound movement. But what was it to start this move?

The holy books say that the universe started with the word "BE": "When He wants something, it suffices that He says 'BE.'"

We cannot comprehend being brought into existence out of nothing, but we can talk about bringing into existence out of what exists.

Being created as His caliph and image, we, too, have the authority to summon the created to ourselves with every word that comes out of our mouth. So, we have the potential to produce a "BE" effect.

In the holy books, the Creator points out to us that the universe was created by simply saying "be" while creating. It is noteworthy that it starts with a word, not any action.

The initiator of the action is sound.

Life is a frequency. The universe communicates through frequencies. Today's technologies use the same system. Every movement has a sound, and every sound has a style of movement. Every syllable that comes out of your mouth initiates a wave of movement.

The word travels towards the new target
like an arrow springing from the bow...
It is the archer who takes aim and draws the bow.

Every frequency emanating from you spreads to every corner of the universe in waves, and as it spreads, it matches with energies and frequencies similar to itself. It returns to the initial address in a timeless interval. What determines the return time of the emitted frequency is the needs and the conscious. If you describe beauty with sweetness, sweet and beautiful things come together. If you convey negativities, pains and evils frequently and with emotions, you will attract the same negativities into your life.

You will meet things that you ask curiously.

Questions can bring expansions or close open doors. As you realize your potential, you will realize the value of silence as much as the power of the word. Questions bear the traces of your quests. You need to pay attention to what you are calling with defiance, reproach, with vibrations of judgment or criticism because you can inadvertently scribble in your book of destiny with your expression pen whereas what each of us wants is that what we write in the book of destiny brings peace. Both your questions and your curiosities have a frequency.

Those asked with judgment and curiosity

1. How did he get it to this state?
2. Why did he go bankrupt?
3. Why would it happen to me?
4. What were you thinking when you did this?

My advice to you is to listen to yourself and the people around you, and be aware of the fateful scribbles that these questions can create. For such questions that you have asked in the past and that you are aware of now, you can convey the necessary message to your subconscious and soften your need to learn with firmness by saying, "I cut off my connection with the questions I have asked with judgment and criticism. May the answers to my questions give me peace of mind."

Expanding question patterns

1. Can I have such a beautiful house, too?
2. Where can I get help to solve this problem?
3. Which books should I read for a successful exam result?
4. 4How can I get help for my body to heal?

It should give you peace of mind when your questions meet their answers. Likewise, the areas where you direct your curiosity also affect your frequency. What are you after, which area do the paths and methods that you follow draw you? Energy fields that include criticism, complaint, gossip and judgment focus you on the negative. Negative is the energies that reduce and pull you down as I mentioned before. Just as an overfilled glass overflows and harms the environment, positive energy can also create negative effects when it goes too far. What lies behind your being inactive on a subject in your life, the decline of your body's energy, or your way of thinking directed to deprivation is these behavior patterns causing energy leaks. Watch yourself. In what rhythm are you in the expressions regarding time and space meetings? Excesses put you away from yourself and cause you to object to the proposals of the universe and want to continue in the same routine. When you insist on keeping your routine the same, you derail from the system which is renewed at any given moment and are thrown into an area you do not want. *Life is harsh to those who resist the flow of the river, and generous to those that flow with it.*

Sameness creates separation.

Misuse of Positive Energy

What turns something into poison is its dose. When you overuse something that is good for you, it can turn into poison. A food you eat excessively can cause allergic reactions in the future. In the case of excessiveness or misuse of the positive energy principle, the following results are likely to occur;

-Not being able to give up things that have been accumulated, even hoarding,

-Continually buying without knowing why, and what it will be used for,

-Excessive desire to control,

-The feeling of tension caused by being controlling,

-Constipation in the intestines,

-Overeating,

-Inability to lose weight,

-Stomach ailments,

-Inability to leave-to break up personal relations,

-Stinginess in material matters,

-Resisting the flow and the course of events,

-Feeling obligated to say yes to everything,

-Controlling people by compromising, altruism,

-Setting unattainable goals in dreams and future plans,

-Doing sports to the extent of torturing the body,

-Overexertion of the body,

-Desire to control others with verbal and written interventions,

-Excessive mental activity,

-Aggression,

-Not being able to stand still,

-Tics,

-Being overly concerned with what is happening around you,

-Negative comments, swearing and cursing about people and events you do not know,

-Being overly critical or judgmental of people who do something you do not approve of.

In life; discussions about politics, quarrels about sports, conflicts over financial matters, excessively watching discussion and gossip programs on television, war and thriller films, programs containing violence, verbal assault, verbal harassment, sexual harassment... they all nourish this area.

Misuse of Negative Energy

In the case of excessiveness or misuse of the negative energy principle, the following results are likely to occur;

-Fear of changing the current order,

-Causing loss to the body due to inactivity,

-Being unable to sleep at night, and waking up very late in the morning,

-Being in a position that is mostly the same throughout the day (at a desk, lying down, in front of the TV, having to stand in the same position professionally, etc.),

-Not being able to set a goal on a subject,

-Not being able to move towards the target,

-Not being able to make decisions on one's own,

-Needing to be managed from outside,

-Constantly protesting,

-Saying "no" to any offer without thinking,

-Not being able to quit a habit,

-Repetitions,

-Talking about the past as if it is today,

-Holding someone else responsible for your experiences,

-Extreme weakness in the body,

-Desiring to lose weight,

-Not being able to breathe,

-Not being able to gain weight,

-Thinking that you are not loved,

-Eating acidic and sugary foods excessively,

-Anemia and blood diseases,

-Circulatory disorders and stagnation of events,

-Intensity in criticism and judging,

-Indolence and procrastination,

-Insisting on buying, finding or doing the exact same thing,

-Curiosities that become mundane,

-Not being able to break from the same-minded social circle,

-Resistance to change,

-Constantly doing the same things throughout the day,

-Staying away from innovation due to fear and anxiety,

-Following an idea, thought or belief with supporter psychology,

-Executing the commands given from outside,

-Idolizing a role model...

Potential for an accident occurs in the area where you overuse positive or negative energy. Balance is restored through sudden energy transfers. Only by maintaining your inner balance can you protect yourself from the need to keep yourself in balance with an external support.

The experiences you define as 'accidents' are actually compelling effects that force you to get out of the current situation and make a new choice: illness as a bodily accident, financial losses as an incidental accident, emotional space accidents, being cheated on and sudden separations. You can also classify in this category the events that are unexpected and that lead you to change the course of your life.

Correct Use of Positive Energy

Positive areas, issues you are in, actions, approaches, and expressions are healing and motivating; they carry you upward and take you forward. When you feel weak, sick and lifeless, you should turn to positive areas. You must have woken up by the time the sun has come, you need to move, use initiating and healing expressions in your expressions, make your own decisions with acceptance of what is going on during the day, and put them into practice with stability.

Correct Use of Negative Energy

Negative areas, issues you are in, actions, approaches, and expressions relax, reduce, slacken, put at ease, excrete and loosen. When you feel tense, controlling, fixed and stressed, you can benefit from negative energy principles. When the sun sets and darkness falls, you need to remain calm, sleep in a dark environment, perform bodily discharges at the right times, and be in acceptance, tranquility, and listening state in your expressions. Getting the right amount of water into the body and not having an acidic diet is also the right use of negative energy.

When you cannot start a change in a certain matter in your life and cannot cut your ties with the old one, you have to find the area where you go to extremes and set your balance. You cannot complain about inertia on the one hand and start anew on the other by continuing the day in the same way you did the previous day as soon as you get up in the morning. Focus on your questions and curiosities, head towards the right area.

Up to this point, we have looked at what area your mind is headed for. Well, have you ever thought about what you are inviting with your dhikr?

Maybe you are repeating such a word without even realizing that the phrase you repeat has led you to experience illness, healing, or transformation.

The science of letters loads information into words.

How about reading the impact of sound frequencies that you think have no meaning?

We hear the emotional effects on the body with audible emotional utterances.

For instance, the sound of sneezing is "Achoo" ("HApşu" in Turkish);

Of coughing "Öhhöhh";

Of pain "Ouch" ("Ahhhh" in Turkish)

Of rage "Öfff"

Of anger "Offf"

Of objection "Üfff"

Of Joy "Hahaha"

The use of the letter "H" with all vowels has a healing effect. In particular, "Ha" and "Hu" are used as a healing sound in heart-related breathing meditation practices. "Ha" and "Ho" are also used in words related to health and healing, such as "hospital," "healing," "hastane," (hospital in Turkish) "heart," etc...

"Ohh – Ahhh – Öhh – Ihh" sounds create a relaxing and therapeutic effect.

"Ha" sound is used to increase the influence of the heart in the body and joy in the emotion.

The extended use of the letter "F" while pronouncing it provides the release of suppressed emotions and the blocked fire of action. The same sound frequency is used as exhaling support while trying to light a fire. Again, the same sound frequency is used when blowing out a candle. It is also used to increase or decrease anger.

The "Fu" sound has a healing and therapeutic effect. In meditation and sound practices, the "Fu" sound is used for kidney health in the body, and to relieve anxiety in the emotion.

The extended use of the letter 'R' radiates a frequency of stubbornness and aggression. With a vowel that follows it, its resistance is broken and it symbolizes spiritual energies.

"Ra, Rahman, Rahim, Ruh, Brahman" (Ruh means soul/ spirit in Turkish)

You, too, realize the power of the words, sounds, and even letters you use in your daily life.

Sometimes, even with a single word coming out of someone's mouth, you can see their mood, the situation they are in, the fate they are and will be living.

How?

For example, let's read together the questions you can ask your friend:

"What's up? How are you?"

"As you know, the market is stagnant, business is slow." / He or she is resisting change, satisfied with things being the same, content with stagnation. His or her business is interrupted.

"We're just getting by." / He or she wants his/her efforts and problems to continue increasing by saying "getting by." (The expression used in the original sentence is not getting by but "rolling"--used in Turkish to say we're getting by--, So, rolling as in the snowball effect will cause the person to continue increasing efforts and problems)

"Thank God everything is fine, may our blessings increase." The events that this grateful person will be grateful for will increase. Things will come to the exact desired level.

"No problem, not bad." / He or she needs a problem. He or she is not satisfied with what is happening, he or she wants to invite problems.

"Markets are bad, no movement at all." / He or she wants to magnify what is bad for himself or herself by focusing on the bad.

"We are thankful even for today." / He or she thinks that he/she is not very happy with his/her life. He or she chooses to live by complaining about events that he/she will not be grateful for by inviting them into his/her life.

"We intend to be with goodness and beauty." / He or she has in the heart that goodness and beauty will find him/her.

"Whatever, it's going." / He or she wants the state of uncertainty and questioning to continue.

"So so!" / He or she is not happy with the situation, he/she wants more, but he/she also knows that he/she will not be given much because he/she is too ambitious...

We read what all these mean through the frequency of the sentence. While making these comments, you should add to your readings the facial expressions and body language of the other person and yours, of course. There is a big difference between a word of gratitude expressed with a grimace or with a smile.

Smiling and saying "no problem" or "no trouble" is an expression of discomfort with the way things are going.

Why does one call distress? He or she calls for such a situation when he/she does not have a future plan, is afraid of the new, and wants to continue his/her routine.

***

Some words and phrases that are either repeated frequently, or almost made into *dhikr*, or not used in the right place secretly convey the real messages.

"Nothing to worry about" means "*There are things that I am watching*" if it's in response to a question. If it is said out of the blue, it means "*I don't care much, but I have concerns.*"

"Not a problem," means that there is a problem unless it is given in response to the question, "Is it a problem?"

"Anyway..." /*It indicates a situation that was imposed despite the person's internal objections.*

"Always the same things, we are used to them now." / To want events and experiences to happen again in the same way; it means chasing after known and customary situations.

"We'll see..." / *It means not being able to act and staring while many events are happening.*

"Let it stay" / It indicates the desire to be fixed, an approach and nature that has difficulty leaving things; and "Let it remain" / It indicates resistance to change when used frequently.

"Just in case…" / Indicates uneasiness.

"Patience…" / Those who use the word patience a lot are those who tend to complicate things.

Just as a bodily form can be formed from a single cell, a destiny can also be created with the root state of a verb.

While expressing, you can push something away thinking you want it, or you can want it to be far away yet bring it closer.

The root of the verb is active in negation words that are not used appropriately and correctly. You think you are expressing what you do not want, but you will see that what you do not want is served to you. Or when someone starts to talk about features that they do not possess, your gaze concentrates on what they express.

"I do not like lying." "I don't want to do any harm." "I do not want to argue with you." "Let's never break up." "I don't like to brag about myself." "I don't want anything to happen to you." "Without accident or mishaps." "Let no sickness, no sorrow come your way." "Let it never spoil." "I don't envy anyone." "Don't be sad in the end." "May God not let us go astray, or let us look to evil people." "May God not let us in the poorhouse."

Negation words can be surely used when they are truly necessary. However, if they are used in out-of-the-blue sentences as in the following examples, they reveal the true intention of the subconscious.

Talking about an accident when there is no accident, or talking about cheating when there is no cheating brings that vibration to life. Of course, it is not in vain that you say it or hear it when it is said. If you are expressing the things that you are worried about happening in your life, you may be expressing your need for that energy.

"I'm afraid something will happen to him." "I am afraid of being wrong." "My only concern is losing." "I will leave you if you cheat on me." "I'll be offended if you do that." "Let's not be together if you're going to upset me." "Be careful that you don't get at odds at the end of this business." Here, the goal of the subconscious is to realize the frequency of the word root.

The pen of destiny is in the tongue,
its effect in the voice.

***

The body, emotions, thoughts, actions, and destiny have formed a harmony with frequently used words, and a common attraction area has been created together.

It is possible to diagnose ailments, diseases, and even experiences by looking at the frequencies of repeated words.

You have a connection with words and sounds that you often repeat in unlikely places. If you pay attention, you will see that even though you have hundreds of options, you always repeat the same words and talk in the same manner. Right now, have a peek into your mind and catch the words you repeat! If you wish, write them on a piece of paper... Let's take a look at what kinds of situations are created with words that are used frequently, whether consciously or not:

If only: You think that what has happened in the past is better and that the present is not good enough. You are of the opinion that your life does not give you pleasure. You are having troubles with the female figures in your life, and your past. You have or are likely to suffer from disorders related to the pancreas and sexual glands.

Ditto/Exactly: If you use these words frequently, you want the past to repeat itself. You imitate rather than use your productive ability, and you need approval. Those who do not want to get out of the repetition cycle use these words quite often. You are likely to experience problems, especially in the back of your body or in the organs on the left.

Definitely/Absolutely: If you use the word 'absolutely' often, you need rigidity and sharpness in your life. You may not yet realize that perfectionism is shallowness. You are just on your way to learning that what happens is best, and you think life is treating you harshly and cruelly. You have the potential to suffer from problems related to the gallbladder, neck, as well as muscle stiffness and knee problems in your life.

The Most/-est: If you use the superlative form frequently, you want to increase a state; compete; quarrel with those around you; surpass others; be ahead; be a favorite; and be approved. You find yourself insufficient and try to hide it from yourself. "I must be the best," Expressions such as "the greatest…", "the strongest…", "the best…" take you away from modesty and increase arrogance. What lies behind this is the sense of inferiority and deficiency. For you, success is a way to prove yourself, to manifest yourself. Especially heartburn ailments are caused by the controlling energy emanating from the frequency of the usage of superlatives.

Nothing: If you use the word 'nothing' often, you basically want to create multiplicity and absence. By the way, I would like to tell an anecdote about the subject.

One day, two men come to Nasreddin Hodja. One complains about the other. The complainant says that he has helped the person next to him, but he could not get what he was promised in return. The man next to him stands with his neck bent and embarrassed. He doesn't even open his mouth.

After the Hodja listens to the complaints long enough, he turns to the silent man and asks, "What promise did you make to this man in return for the help he gave you?"

"Nothing," the man says.

Thereupon, Nasreddin Hodja responds, "Is it true?" he asks.

"Right," says the man. "He didn't give me the 'nothing' he promised."

Hodja lifts the end of the rug and says to the complaining man, "Take what's under here." The man does as he is told and reaches under the rug with his hand. But there is nothing there.

"What's in your hand?" asks Hodja. "Nothing," he replies. Hodja answers wittily:

"Now you got nothing. Write off each other's debt and go."

In short, 'Nothing' is the energy of absence.

Always: If you use the word 'always' frequently, you want to continue repetitions and stagnation in your life. You have a routine life. There is monotony in the area where this expression is used. Where there is routine, there is mediocrity and a lack of pleasure.

A relationship in which you say, "Let's always be together!" continues with the residues or traces left behind even after the separation in the next relationship because the togetherness is not over yet and it 'always' continues. When you express that you want your family to always be together, you cannot cut them out of your life even when you realize that they harm you because, with your statement, you have approved of being 'always together'.

There are traces of the need for multiplicity and pluralism in the words 'all' and 'all of us'.

But: If you use the word 'but' often, you are an objector on the inside. You cannot silence the part of you that says "I know."

Since what you know governs you, you are closed to new things and to taking. And because you do not get what is on offer, you cannot let go of the old either. You are likely to experience constipation and intestinal problems.

Come on, immediately, quickly: If you use these words frequently, you think you are delaying or postponing the steps you need to take. Your subconscious is right about this. You are slowing yourself down by acting hastily in different areas, simply because you cannot see on what subject you are lingering. You pretend to be in a hurry, using these words often, until you find the areas where you procrastinate and decide to move forward in them. People of this nature are especially likely to develop heart-related disorders in their bodies.

There is not: If you use the phrase 'there is not' frequently, you are calling the absence of something in your life. You may not be able to take, resist taking most of the time, or even despise it.

Never: If you are using the word 'never' frequently, you are inviting yourself to what you really need to do. When you say, "I'll never go, I'll never do…", they are for you to remember what you really need to do. You cannot escape what you really need to do. Whichever of your friends says, "I will never get married!", it means you will be going to that friend's wedding first.

Those who use the word 'never' frequently experience problems in their knees and neck due to compression and an inability to bend. In addition, they may experience gall bladder problems.

More: If you use the word 'more' often, you are producing dissatisfaction. You cannot be satisfied with what is already there, you think that it is not enough. As you feel insufficient and incomplete, you think that no matter what is given to you,

you will not be able to meet the goal you set. Therefore, you can experience shortness of breath, tightness in your chest, weight problems, dissatisfaction, and hormone imbalances. It also means that you want to make your greed and ego grow in a negative way.

I know: You are closed to knowing what you do not know and to the new. It is a phrase that is frequently used in cases of attachment to the old. It is one of the biggest obstacles to learning and awareness.

Enough: It is a word used to terminate, complete and end something in an area, and it can suddenly stop the flow in an area in your life. If you use it too often, you have resistance and problems with receiving. Your shelves or capacity may be insufficient for what is offered.

Maybe: It is the state of not being able to see the uncertainty and calculations of probabilities clearly and not being able to make a full decision. Frequent use causes indecisiveness.

Right/"Isn't it?": It is said due to the need to seek the approval of the outside and others. If it is used frequently, it can reduce willpower and weaken the will.

Later: It is often said to postpone. When used frequently, it is understood that what is being postponed is the plan for the future because the person is constantly postponing himself/herself and his/her life.

Sir/Madam: Since childhood, you may have been taught to use the word 'sir/madam' when talking to your elders. However, in their literal meaning, it is known that the 'sir/madam' is above, the one who calls him/her 'sir/madam' is below and serves the one above. This is a sign of servitude and the need to be used.

Pardon me: This expression is used as a kind way of asking someone to repeat what they have said. However, not being able to hear or catch what has been said does not necessitate a 'pardon'. Saying "pardon me", rather than "Could you repeat that?" or "I couldn't hear you" indicates the sense of inferiority of the listener to the speaker, thus creates a sense of unworthiness.

OK: If you say 'ok' to everything that is said, you cannot distinguish between what is useful and what is harmful to yourself. You feel unprotected because you cannot draw your own ego boundaries and you cannot say 'no' to curry favor with others.

From now on/no longer: Even in businesses that you think you are just starting, you want to leaven the past and repeat the energies of the past and look back. For this reason, you always leave 'leftover' and incomplete work from the past.

I have to/I need to: If you frequently use the phrases 'I have to' and 'I need to', you need stimulation and to be nudged to work and move forward. Your obligation is your captivity, your bondage. It would be wise to be careful about the cardiovascular system.

I sacrificed: If you use the word 'sacrifice' often, you have embraced the victim role too much. You are trying to gain profit from your suffering. People with this nature have a high probability of suffering from rheumatism.

I want so much: If you keep repeating that you want something 'very much', that thing you want will not happen. Why is that? Because saying 'much' actually turns here into saying 'There is no.' You do not want something 'so much', you 'just want' something; and when you place that order, it happens... The reason you choose to go to extremes with 'much' is due to the frequency of uncertainty. This is actually a state of pretending to want. You use the word 'so much' to push what you want a little further away from you. 'Wanting too much' is actually deceiving oneself. Underneath the expression "I want it so much, but it doesn't happen" lies the thought, "I don't want it and it wouldn't make me happy if it happened."

I'm afraid: If you use the phrase 'I'm afraid' frequently, you need to be protected and to be driven with fear. For this reason, the probability of experiencing disorders in the adrenal glands and blood diseases increases. There may also be trouble with rooting in life. Rooting issues cause profanity or the use of vulgar words in speech. Blackness under the eyes and kidney diseases are also related to this.

For instance, you say, "I'm afraid of getting stuck in the elevator!" Don't worry, you may come across an elevator that will break down just when you are in it. And when you say, "Then I'll never take the elevator, problem solved," you will either be locked in a dark room or a place where the key has been lost, so you will have met the reflection of your fear at one point.

What Do Frequently Told Memories Tell?

Memories that you have lived in the past and that you often tell today are not things you mention for no reason. It does not matter whether you are talking about a childhood experience or an old relationship...

I want you to watch yourself from the outside as you recount the memories you repeat. You will realize that you are transferring that memory to others with the effect of that moment as if you are reliving it.

Until you learn the lesson that the event in the memory is trying to convey to you, it is natural to retell the same event from the same angle. Your subconscious knows that you need to invite the events you describe or other situations of similar frequency into your life once again.

Then it is possible to say this;

Those who repeat their memories actually want to relive the same experience once more and continue in that 'state'.

For example, if you are still narrating an event you experienced as a child with the same feelings of those years, from the eyes of your child self, then you do not want the child inside you to grow up. If you can look through that child's eyes and make evaluations based on the knowledge of the state you have reached today, it means that you are progressing.

A relative of mine used to constantly complain about her husband when he was alive. She used to tell me that her husband had harmed her and turned her life into a living hell. Shortly after her husband died, she started to complain about her brother and son. According to the woman, only people on the outside, but especially the men were guilty, and she was the victim. More and more, people around her distanced themselves from her. So, the woman devoted her life to praying. She was almost out of touch with everyone, and despite this, she kept complaining.

Remember that every word that comes out of the mouth creates a vibration and this vibration initiates an action. The system has taken your command to perform the frequencies of your words. The main reason why this woman turned away from life to worship was that the words of complaint that came out of her mouth smeared on her and polluted her heart. She was praying too much in order to be purified and to start being in acceptance although she did not know she had defiled herself in the past.

Since she still looked at her old self while telling her memories and could not be in acceptance, her complaints about her experiences with her husband were also reflected in her relationship with other men in her life. However, if she could have gotten the message of what she experienced, she would have freed herself and lived the rest of her time happily, instead of battling what she saw in the mirror. Look again at the bonds you have established with your memories with today's awareness, see the contribution of your experiences to you, and end the cycle of repetition in your memories.

> *Every word that comes out of your mouth*
> *seals the deal for a wish.*

Always remember that you are part of a system that serves you, without sorting out what comes out of your mouth. Your wishes are presented to you as they are. The system does not distinguish which request is positive and which one is negative. The one who asks is given what he/she wants.

Songs, jokes, movies you watch, belief patterns, memories constantly told... Know that every statement is recorded and the order is completed. With these records, you decide what you want, what you tend to do, and which way you will turn.

Routines are the fuel of the repeating cycle.
"I hope I won't get sick."
"May things not go wrong."
"May our relationship not turn sour."
"I don't want any trouble."

Although these expressions may seem well-intended, they are actually focused on what is not wanted rather than what is wanted.

Sick – wrong – sour – trouble...

These words in the sentences are actually calls and invitations registered in the system.

It is vital that you focus on what you want, not what you do not want... Therefore, do not only stop talking about events that you do not want to happen or that you do not want to experience a similar one, but also stop watching such events. May your words give you peace as they come from your mouth towards your life.

Life is a perfect table where all kinds of beautiful states, situations, encounters, and reflections are presented to you. When you take one fruit from that table and say, "Oh how delicious!" after tasting it, you become integrated with that taste. You can continue to experience the same tastes with this witnessing. Sometimes you also start posing questions: "How does that happen? Why does this taste like this? Why is it red?"

As you ask questions, new tables begin to be set in order to give you answers. For example, let's suppose that while hearing the noise coming from the neighbor's house, you start asking questions such as: "How do they make so much noise?", or "Is this how a man treats his wife?", or "Why does he drink so much?" From that moment on, a new table is set where you will leave the state of the witness and receive the answers to your questions. Because your words and wishes are so important that even the questions you ask are shown to you in your own life to be answered. While the fate you create with sincere and genuine questions asked with the intention of learning would give you pleasure; your questions filled with complaints, judgments and criticism, you may encounter answers that you will not like so much.

Surely, the moment of uttering an expression, its frequency of occurrence is not coincidental. You are using that expression because of a need that is written in your potential. Any 'word' that comes out of your mouth will definitely come true, even if you cannot know where it will wind up. Even if you cannot understand where an event has come from when or after you experience it, even if you object by saying, "I didn't actually want this experience that way, that's not what I said," what you experience is entirely a request originated from you. The system works with such perfect mathematics that everything it delivers to you is made up of your calls.

You may experience financial turbulence sometimes, or an emotional experience, or a physical problem, and you may ask yourself, "Where did this come from?" Your objections may continue until you realize the destination that this event you are experiencing has taken you to. However, once you realize that the order is yours and say, "I'm glad it happened this way," and accept that what has happened is the best way, you will save yourself from the repetition cycle.

Here are the words I often hear when this topic comes up in our workshops:

"Why would anyone want to experience economic hardship?"

"What now, was it I who wanted to be sick?"

"Did I ask to be fired?"

You may also object to the fact that the events that you think you do not want in your life are actually your own order. So, how would you like if we stopped here and read together the before-actual-after states of what happened with a sample event?

Let's say you went to visit a friend and when you saw how happy he is at his job and how much he enjoys what he does, you were very enticed and said, "Let me also have my own business so that I'll be happy while doing it." But at the time, you were working as an assistant manager in a company. Your manager was making you feel good, your salary was quite high and you were living very comfortably. After a while, you notice that strange things start to happen at work, you feel under intense pressure, but you continue to compromise. You go to a job interview or two, but the financial conditions are worse than the job you currently have and you decide to stay at your job. The environment you work in is gradually getting tense and you feel obligated to quit your job. You are looking for a job again, not knowing what to do. However, all doors are closing in your face, your compensation is about to run out and you are rebelling now. Your friends do not call as often as they used to, your family turns their back on you, you get lonely. You get the feeling that you are moving in the opposite direction on the highway. You panic and you become obligated to take a job much further from home and settle for half of your old income. In a smaller company, you make money by doing the work of more than one person.

You are now at the stage where objections begin.

"Why did this happen to me?"

"What did I do to deserve this?"

But when exactly did it start?

Of course, with the order that you gave, by emulating your happy friend who has set up his own business, to live in that state ...

What did the system do?

First of all, it created the conditions where you can quit your job in which you felt worthless. When you did not volunteer for it, it forced you to quit your job. You valued the old and could not easily let go because you wanted to follow the old one.

Thus, your support and resources decreased. Until then, you were working for money. But what was it about your friend that you emulated? His happiness and his state of feeling worthy...

Your friend has also traveled several paths and has been through various stages until he has found the happiness he is experiencing. You only saw the result he obtained... However, the system sees the whole picture, takes action to bring you to that result, prepares you for the same result, and starts teaching you the various lessons you need to learn in order to achieve the result you desire. You are now a student of the 'Be happy in your own job' school. This means that you need to study until you graduate from school. As long as you remember the past, you will freeze your enrollment and delay your graduation.

So, does the new always come with difficulties?

When you are able to distance yourself from doubts and trust that what you want will be given to you easily, you will obtain the new easily and quickly.

As long as you keep clutching your ties to the old,
new experiences will cause you to fall...

Remember that you said, "I'm glad this has happened" in the process of change after you encountered the results of the things you objected to and resisted.

People whose bodies become ill may learn to prioritize and value their health; those who experience financial stress may learn to take action by relying on themselves and their abilities; those who become unemployed may learn the value of working and manage to get better, or all of these people feel nostalgia to their old self and complain more. After all, what is given to you is what you need. On the other hand, if you resist the event you have invited, things can get out of control.

Contracts of Fate

The expression "A word once spoken is past recalling" told to a person who does not keep his/her word is not an idiom that has been established in the language in vain. Even if it is not put in writing, we do not feel comfortable when we cannot keep our promises. The system we are a part of works on the same principle.

A promise is a contract,
and only a new contract can change this contract.

You may have knowingly or unknowingly made various agreements with the people or things in your life through your words.

"I will never leave you."

"We will always stay together."

"I have a memory of him that I will keep for the rest of my life."

"Money corrupts me."

"I've worked so hard, I can't quit..."

These expressions can be counted as examples that we can give to contracts of fate. Even if it is someone else who is speaking the words, when you say "yes" to each one of them, you are also confirming the contract. You now have your signature, too, under these words.

Maybe you are looking at life from a different perspective right now, you may not be supporting the words you signed, but a bargain is a bargain because a word once spoken is past recalling. The system has already received your approval of the words you disapprove of today.

A counselee of mine kept complaining about not having a stable relationship. She recalled that she had frequently used expressions such as "You will always be in my heart, I will never forget you, I will only be with you forever" while making plans for the future with her boyfriend in college. Through these words she signed at that time, she actually made a contract of fate with her lover. Since she had not yet fully broken the deal from within, she had unwittingly kept her words. Finally, she noticed this bond and decided to cut it. She sat down as if her ex was in front of her and said, "I'm terminating all the deals I made with you. I'm opening my door to the new and unfamiliar..."

Thus, she closed the door on the old one.

When you realize that you have been calling out the compelling or unwanted experiences in your life with your words, you gain the power to transform them once more with your words.

Fate Invited to Life through Jokes and Songs

The fastest and most effective areas of 'creation' take place in moments when the mind is at its calmest. During these moments, even the lyrics you hum are accepted as an order by the system as your special wishes and desires.

For example, when you listen to breakup songs, you may experience separation agony. The periods when you listened to cheerful and happy songs may have been the time of your most enjoyable experiences. When you notice which songs people around you listen to frequently, you can easily predict what kind of event they may experience in the future. Even if you warn them not to listen to songs with negative lyrics, you may find that they do not pay attention to you because they need the destiny created with that frequency of words in songs and jokes.

Even words that are expressed without emphasis and sentences that are only used as a joke are taken into account by the system. For example, excuses for illness made up for not going to class may shortly come true as an experience of illness.

Vicious Circles

Because of the words you use habitually and frequently, you can create chains of events that repeat continuously. The way to get rid of this vicious circle that you have created with your own expressions is to comprehend the reason for your need to use those words and what you have created in your life through them.

It is necessary to detect the recurring events and the statements that call these events in order to get out of the vicious circle. Then you can change the events you experience by choosing your statements in the direction you want your life to take. Sometimes just a word changes and transforms life.

Reading Events

The events we experience define us to ourselves. The characters, situations, behaviors and attitudes of the people we meet are also related to us. In other words, your encounters, problems, diseases, accidents, coincidences, possessions, and what you witness in your life belong entirely to you.

The events you experience and witness in your life originate from your own center. You are the cause of every event, and every event is there to tell you something. Think of life as a scene in a movie: you have written the script with your thoughts and directed it with your words. You are in the leading role with your body. The reflections around you are also supporting roles that you have tailored and distributed according to your own needs. Maybe you are watching the cinema of life that you have created from your existence and reflected from yourself as if you are watching someone else's movie. The moment you realize that you are the person sitting in the director's chair, you begin to own the story. While this awareness makes you responsible for the choices you make, it also encourages you to use the power you possess correctly.

In every event you experience, put yourself at the center of the event, and focus on what the event wants to tell you. When you read the events correctly, you can come up with solutions and use the pen of your destiny for your wishes.

Events also have their own language of narration. This language is sometimes expressed in colors, shapes, behaviors, and symbols. For example, if you did not realize and solve something that was told to you about your father in your childhood, it will be told to you through another man, authority, laws, or your son in the years to come. In the same way, something that was told to you about your mother in your childhood, if you did not realize the information you need to get and solve it, can be told to you in the years to come through your body, memories, relationships, or financial issues. We can read the unity of life with the principle of duality (dual balance).

For example, someone who is trying to commute by his car is hit from behind by someone else in traffic. Let's say the right brake light of the car was broken in this accident. He is also late for work because of the accident.

Let's look at this incident together:

The car – It is the person's view of life and reality.

The back of the car – It is the person's history.

The right rear of the car – The person's relationship with his father, his life plans in the past.

The fact that the brake light is broken – It is the person's attempt to stop the flow of events because of the future plans he did in the past.

So, this accident tells that the person has resisted and rebelled against the laws of life and authority in the events he has experienced.

To wrap up, the person cannot set new goals for himself, he cannot progress and stops his development because he resists changing the future plans he has made with the knowledge and experience inherited from his father. Therefore, we can say that he is experiencing setbacks in his work.

While reading the events, put yourself in the center and place the symbols in the table I have given. Focus closely on what the outcome tells you as if you are completing a puzzle.

***

Let's say a child riding a bicycle is hit by a car and people around run to help the child. The incident has different effects for the driver of the car, for the doctor who has come to help the child, for the mother of the child, the pregnant woman who has witnessed the accident, and the child who has had the accident.

After an incident has happened, it remains only at the moment when you received its knowledge. The knowledge you have accumulated until then can affect your judgments, connection with the incident, and your point of view. You make a transfer to your future according to your approach to the incident. The system presents the judgment as a cake to those who give up witnessing and are willing to be involved; the same cake is served to them over and over as long as they eat from that cake. For those who received the information of the incident by remaining as a witness, life made them watch this experience in the mirror of the incident so that they could decide what they did not want.

So, what is the knowledge of this case?

For the driver who caused the accident to happen; *he may decide to quit being careless and hurrying due to his regret of the incident. Or, on the contrary, he may blame the child for suddenly appearing in front of him, and his mother for not looking after the child.*

For the child involved in the accident; *he may learn from this incident which happened to him because he acted carelessly, and decide to act carefully from then on. Or, he may ignore this event, cannot receive the information of the incident, and carry the shock of the accident with him. He can also add this event to the memories that he repeats. He may feel guilty, remorseful, discouraged, and may become timid and cowardly. He may become someone who only does what he is told.*

For the mother of the child in the accident; *in this incident, she may see the mistakes she has made while educating her child, learn the lesson of the incident, and decide to direct her child correctly. She may also reach a completely different conclusion from this incident: she blames herself, blames the driver, blames her husband who does not support her in child care, even her child who has had the accident. She may continue to get angry about what has happened. She can talk about this accident often and create a vicious circle because she has not learned the lesson of the incident.*

For the pregnant woman who saw the accident; *she can decide what not to do while raising her children.*

For those who judge the accident; *for those who stop being a witness to the event and differentiate the parties involved as right* *or wrong, their perspective at the event will leave different traces on their future. Witnesses of an event, those who live and hear it, are also the inviters of that event. We all have a part in every event that happens, even one in seven billion.*

You cannot change what happened in the past, but you can transform yourself by changing your connection with the incident you lived, and your perspective towards it. The past does not change, it remains the same, yet its effect on you changes. Here lies the key to healing many phobias and traumas.

You, too, may have witnessed many people who separated their experiences from themselves and blamed the outside, leaving their places, jobs, relationships, and even countries. The job was changed, the spouse was changed, the house was changed, but the thing that was seen as a problem and fled from was carried on their back to the place they went.

I had a friend who was too sensitive about cleanliness. One day, he said, "There is no hygiene in this city. Istanbul is not a clean city. Everywhere, everything is full of germs..." he said, meaning that there is a serious cleaning problem in Istanbul. As it turns out, he did his own research and decided that among the countries he had visited, the cleanest and most hygienic life was in Singapore. "Everything is great there," he said, "very clean. An almost germ-free country..."

He said he would travel to Singapore again in a few weeks. I said to him, "As long as you can't figure out this cleanliness thing in your head, you'll carry this problem with you wherever you go."

Shortly after he left for Singapore, the country was quarantined for the bird flu virus.

My friend called me months later, "Do you know what has happened to me?" he said, "We can't go out because of the bird flu. Even at home, we walk around with masks. I want to decide to go back to Turkey, but we can't even go to the airport because of the quarantine. Those good old cats, germs, land... I miss Istanbul so much." Shortly after returning to Turkey, cleanliness was no longer an obsession for him and it became a normal thing.

All kinds of situations that seem to be unrelated to each other in the events you have experienced and that you have difficulty in relating to one another are actually part of a web knitted with invisible threads. Nothing happens for no reason or by chance.

While the universe makes the demands and wishes of each of us real on our behalf, it works in an enormous order in endless variations.

Messages in Economic Events

The root of the problems experienced in material matters is actually hidden in the perspective that you have acquired and maintained in the past, related to the body, money, and the way you communicate with women.

When you treat your body harshly, you feel indebted to your body. When you categorize women, when you judge the body of another person, when you judge the value you give to that body and those around you in accordance with their power and financial situation, you are in debt to them; and when you feel gratitude or hope for someone's help, you are indebted to your own life plan.

Especially in the bond you formed with your mother, whether or not she feeds you enough, makes you feel safe or not, approves or disapproves of you and what you do determine the course of your economic situation. If your bond with your mother is healthy, you will be in financial prosperity. If not, you will continue to attract these financial problems into your life. When you focus on any of the examples I have listed so far and find the source of the problem and solve it, change begins in all other areas as well.

Practice:

Make a plan in order to consider how such a plan will contribute to your approach to women and your relationships with them, and will improve these. Whenever you find an issue by which you judge women, you should abandon this area. Remember that your approach to women vibrates at the same frequency as your approach to your own body and life.

What could be your solutions?

1. You can contribute to a girl's education.
2. You can facilitate a woman's daily workflow.
3. You can buy a gift and praise a woman whom you have judged or gossiped about before.
4. You can make peace with women, including all the women who have entered your life. You can free yourself from your sides that are fighting with them and reach a compromise.

Practice:

If you judge your own body and the bodies of others, you can do some exercises to improve your perspective. Your approach to your body, to women and to matter have similarities.

1. Switch to a healthy diet. Take care of your body with the awareness of what is beneficial and harmful for you in the food you will offer to your body.
2. Take physical action. Wake up early in the morning and greet the day with vigor and hugs.
3. Take a walk every day for your health.
4. Remember that activating your body with exercises means initiating movement in other areas of your life as well.
5. Identify the points in your body that your breath does not reach and send them oxygen by unclogging them.
6. Balance your sleep and work rhythm.
7. Take care of not only your own body but also others' bodies and health.
8. Love your body and be kind to it.

You may be questioning the connection between financial issues and the body and relationships with women. However, each one is part of a common frequency... In holistic medicine, acne on the skin indicates liver fattening. There is no difference between cleansing the liver to get rid of acne and establishing the balance between physical and economic conditions.

Look carefully at 'what has happened'... It always tells the truth.

The name of the sum of what you have experienced, watched, and felt so far is WHAT HAS HAPPENED. All of them have come to life with your verbal requests and your approval. So, we can say this: what has happened always tells the truth because it has been shaped according to your real need and situation. Although the mind refuses this with various excuses, our work and experience to date have shown that we have our own share in the events that each of us invites into our lives. When you read any event with the principle of "What has happened tells the truth," you will see that you get very precise and surprising results.

***

A child who is laughing and playing with joy becomes the center of attention of everyone. It nurtures those around it with its activity and joy. Feeling happy, being cheerful has a magnetic effect. It is no different than a magnet. When the child cries for no reason and disobeys, the attention and approval it receives change as well. The magnetic effect formed around the child reverses and switches to repulsion. When the child cannot express its needs and its crankiness is not replaced with satisfaction, it disrupts both its own peace and those around it.

We all become happy when our needs are met, our frequency improves, an attraction towards us begins. The vibration emitted by the emotion you are experiencing determines what will come towards you and what will go away from you. The fragrance of the flowers and the invitingness of their colorful images invoke joy, cheer, and a state of serenity, safety, certainty, and beauty as a frequency, which is a healing interaction.

***

Loud voices, angry attitudes, exasperation, pessimism, grief, aggressive attitudes, and anxiety-provoking events urge you to go away.

The state of being happy is the moment when your needs are met and you come up with a solution. Failure to meet needs breeds anger, resentment, and objections. However, the system always meets the demands. It is important to identify what you need, but even more important is to be able to accept what you want when presented to you. When you cannot meet what you demand, resistance builds up inside you. This resistance is the intimidating aspect of what you have learned, your past experiences, emotional connections, and novelties. The new is the abandonment of the old although you call out the new. You have a desire to stay in the past in the areas that you cannot renew. Your mind may want to persuade you that you are not attached to the old and you may say, "I demand it, but it doesn't happen." You can also say, "I experience all that I don't want," and object to what is happening and the system.

If you have a destructive feeling inside about any subject, you have objections to that subject. If you have objections, there are things that you cannot accept. Your consent is required by the system to nurture you and deliver your needs exactly the way you want them to. Another name for this approval is acceptance.

When you read the message of what is presented correctly and remove the resistance, things you say, "That would be great..." will come true, too.

A child who cries because of hunger must first stop crying and calm down before he is able to eat. In your case, you accepting what is reflected from you means that you are calmed down.

***

One of my consultees was unhappy about being overweight. All she wanted was to get slim and look nice. She could not take responsibility for the emotions, moods, and behaviors that are responsible for her weight. She was expecting me to do some magic and get her fit without her moving from her place. She could not accept the reasons that brought her to this state, and object to what had happened. Together, we reviewed her behavioral patterns and eating patterns. We found that when she felt under pressure and could not escape from it, she could not control her urge to eat, and that she constantly consumed sweets because she could not enjoy life. She also admitted that she ate with a rage that she could not control as if she was getting revenge. Her diet and physical problem pointed to her mother. In symbolism, the mother represents material issues and productivity. When considered from this point of view, it was revealed that she was dependent on her family for financial matters, and she did not dare to get a job on her own because she was afraid of losing the comfort her family offered.

Although her request was about her desire to get thinner, what she really and exactly wanted was a career in which she would freely express herself using her talents. In the following weeks, she started to lose weight rapidly. At first, she could not understand the reasons why she was losing weight, she thought it was me.

"It was because you had the courage to face your fears," I said, "You've let your repressions come to light, now if you're ready to step out of that comfort zone you're used to and spread out, you can take off this 'weight coat' you're wearing for protection. All of this was made possible by your decision to open the door to the system for your transformation. It is your will that opens the door and initiates miracles. Now you are even freer in the steps you will take to slim down and unlock your own talents." She followed the nutrition and detox programs I gave her to heal her body to the letter. She walked regularly every day, and did various sports that stretched her body, started to love it, and as she relieved the pressure on her body, she got rid of her extra weight.

Her belief in herself and the system allowed her talents to surface. Miracles came one after another as she unleashed her talents. She has now become a well-known and respected person in her field. With her own skills, she reached a much better comfort level than her family had provided her with.

When reading events about yourself and those around you, focus on what need the current situation meets at that moment. See the connections that have brought things to this point. Remember that there is a beginning for every result. When you bring the result and the beginning together, you will be able to see the whole picture. If you want to change the outcome, you can find the source it feeds on and change its direction or cut the connection.

Reading Emotions

The emotions you feel define yourself to you. Whatever the emotions and states you are experiencing are, they create the vibrations that emanate from you. The traces of these vibrations determine what you invite into your life. While the emotions blowing like a warm breeze create a feeling of relief around you, the emotions blowing with the harshness of a hurricane clutter your surroundings.

Sometimes while someone is talking, you smell anger; and sometimes while listening to someone, you feel their fear. Even though the fight has not started yet, its winds have started to blow around. In other words, there is an invitation to conflict in the speech of the parties. Just as people embracing each other can make others feel the vibration of longing, the anxiety of a mother who is looking for her lost child is reflected in those around her.

There are broadcasts you make with the frequency of the emotion you radiate when you ask questions like "Why am I experiencing these?" or "Why can't I improve my life?"

There are negative thought patterns behind what you invite into your life with your voice that cracks and croaks while emanating the frequency of anger. When you think that you want something good for your life, such an expression pops up that it can destroy everything. Your emotional frequency will prevent you from seeing what you are experiencing due to the smoke coming from the fire of anger.

What you want with the vibration of fear can attract what you fear to happen into your life. Your broadcast shouts "Fear!" As you become unable to distinguish between the useful and the useless, your kidneys, ears or bones will also be adversely affected by the frequency you emit. Once you realize which events and diseases the emotion frequency emanating from you attracts into your life, you can either choose to improve or maintain the current situation.

In a forest fire, if you only focus on fire, and ignore the trees and the air that feeds it, you cannot put out the fire.
You will lose your resources, especially your time and effort for this cause.
When you eliminate the elements that feed the fire in order to put it out, your battle with fire is over.
You will be free from the consequences you do not want.

If an incident makes you angry, the feeling of anger will come back to you after it leaves you. Just like a boomerang... But remember that it will come by collecting and multiplying the like. Once you realize the source and cause of anger and use the license to bend that energy, then it is possible to talk about a real transformation. In short, the moment you realize what is happening, you no longer need that emotional bond.

Where there is anger, there is smoke and the smoke prevents you from seeing yourself, not allowing you to move forward and to feel love. Because you cannot see yourself and feel love, a need for approval would arise for you. You would want to be under other people's control in order to be approved and move forward. The outside becomes more important than you. This is some kind of being herded. As you move away from your own center, from the bond of love, anger increases, and a vicious circle forms. Once you realize that you are governed by your emotions, that is when you will see why you experience the incidents that you involuntarily experience, and you will be able to end them.

You may have some negative emotion addictions that have formed due to your traumas and have started to rule you. That is why, it is so important to focus on the expressions you use to describe yourself and your environment. As long as you say, "It is so", rest assured that it will go on the same way. You can only bring about transformation by changing your expressions and behavior patterns.

If you use the following statements often while defining yourself, you should know that you have fixed attitudes in your emotions that influence your decisions. As you continue to use these expressions, the listed situations that you express will increase in your life.

"I get angry when..."

"I get cross..."

"I get mad..."

"I won't forgive him if he does that."

"Whatever I say…"

"I'd feel upset...."

"I'd feel sorry for..."

"I hate when..."

"I get annoyed when..."

"I cannot bear..."

"It drives me crazy..."

"I'd be devastated..."

Practice:

Listen to yourself for seven days, jot down the words you repeat often.

Identify what you attract into your life with the words you use frequently and write them down. Decide on the ones you want to let go of.

Do an expression fasting for twenty-one days. When the phrases you have detoxed yourself from come out of your mouth involuntarily, stay quiet for ten minutes and rest your expression. At the end of twenty-one days, watch your detoxed state for seven days. Write down the changes you have gone through in your notebook. Compare where you started with where you ended up. Appreciate your success.

Simplify Your Expressions So That Your Life Gets Better.

Positive emotions have the same power of attraction as negative emotions. That is, positive energies such as joy, excitement, happiness gather gratifying events and people. If you produce happiness, if you smile, you attract happy energies into your life. Whatever your potential is, the gravitational force your potential will create is the same. Sincerity or insincerity is noticed not only by us but also by the system.

The product of someone who intends to heal is happiness.

If there is heaven inside, it will be heaven outside. Heaven is not presented to you by some people. It is a state experienced inside and you carry this state wherever you go. It does not matter whether you change country or continent. You take yourself wherever you go. The energy you project follows you wherever you are.

If you can see for what reasons and in what areas what energies and emotions you have created, by noticing yourself, this gives you the 'right to transform' as you see them.

Our behavior and actions originate from our states and moods. What we experience inside is also what we will be reflecting in our dreams. Whatever emotions we experience inside, our reactions to external events, and our expressions that come out of our mouths are related to this. That is why, when we transform ourselves, our situation, our emotions, and the reflections of our emotions, our life begins to transform.

Various fluctuations occur with the pull of positive or negative emotions. Being controlling, fluctuations of sadness, grief, fear, and anxiety may negatively affect not only the aura, energy body, vibrations, and thoughts but also the body. When the emotions are calm, there is peace. When you establish your perceptions and concepts in life; when you can reach the state of witnessing through your realizations; when you can reach the rank of the witness, your states and situations mature. By transmitting what you have started in the body to life, events, and emotions, you can bend your bond with what is. This way, you can start the transformation.

Practice:

Implement a one-month change program with the 'reduce-increase' system and follow what is happening in both your body and your emotions. At the beginning, write down your intention on the first day and make an evaluation at the end of one month.

"I intend that my body, my health and my life to get better."

Week 1
Remove bakery products from your diet for a week. Substitute them with protein foods.

Week 2
Eliminate sugar and all sugar-added foods from your life. Consume one apple a day instead.

Week 3
Eliminate animal food from your diet. Increase the amount of legumes, grains and vegetables.

Week 4
Exclude meat products, milk and dairy products completely from your nutrition program. Opt for olive oil, raw vegetables and fruit instead.

At the end of four weeks, feed on only liquids for one full day. Eat grain-free soups; drink vegetable juices, water and herbal teas.

Practice:

Get up half an hour early in the morning. Walk for fifteen minutes, stretch for fifteen minutes. If there is no opportunity to take a walk outside, open the window and practice stretching. Take a deep breath. Let the oxygen you inhale reach every inch of your lungs.

Sit in a quiet place for three minutes each morning and evening. Open your eyes and watch the surroundings without moving, without comment, without judgment. If you wish, you can extend this non-judgmental witnessing period for a few more minutes.

Get a measuring cup to keep track of the amount of water you drink throughout the day. Increase water and herbal tea consumption. Reduce your consumption of coffee and acidic liquids.

In a quiet environment at night, close your eyes for five minutes, put your hands on your heart and listen to the rhythm. Turn to yourself, your heart beating under your hands, and the one who makes that heartbeat, open yourself to his love.

Take a day for yourself. Drink plenty of water, rest, and listen to your inner voice.

Love is the Source of Happiness, the Channel of Existence of Life

Love is embracing life. It is a state of being, meeting, and it is the nutrition for the continuity of life. As you witness the mechanisms of nature and life; as you see the flowers making themselves beautiful to attract bees; as you watch how the same flowers take form in the nature they feed when they die, and as you watch how every ending gives birth to a beginning, you meet with the Creator. You open yourself up to that flow and the inclusivity of love. When you turn your head to goodness and beauty outside, your faith in the healing and transforming of your life increases.

To increase your love energy, spend time with children, answer their questions, participate in the games they play, let your inner child emerge, be with happy and smiling people, have a blooming flower in your home. Smile and greet yourself every time you go in front of the mirror. When you encounter a problem that you cannot solve alone, focus on the solution, solve that issue in your imagination and trust the system; send your thought to the universe like a cloud and be sure that that cloud will bring a rain of solutions.

Improvement Practice

When you detect any discomfort in an organ or a problem in your life, you should first express that you intend to leave this troubled state. Sit in a quiet place where you can be alone, close your eyes, and focus on your breathing for a few minutes. Take deep breaths. Put a smile on your lips. Let all your facial muscles relax. While your lips give a quiet laugh, you focus on your eyes and smile with your eyes. Bring the laughter in your eyes to your heart. Every time your heart beats, let the laughter inside your veins flow, and the blood in your veins carry the smile throughout your body. As your face and heart laugh with laughter, this state is reflected in your whole body. Then focus on the organ you want to heal, send your inner smile to him so it can join in this laughter.

Dreams are a symbolic language used by the universe.

Reading Life Over Dreams

The dream is the reporting of knowledge in the core of the states, situations, expressions, and events you live on earth to your soul and essence with the language of the universe and a symbolic language.

In other words, a dream is an interpretation you contribute to what you experience.

The interpretation of your life is your dreams.

The message of the dream is to the dreamer; no matter who you see in the dream, first of all, they send a message to you.

So how does the dream occur?

Let's say you went to the market and bought various vegetables. You will cook for the evening with the things you have bought. Of course, what you will add to your meal will not only be the vegetables you have bought from the market. Spices, salt and more will go into it. In other words, the meal will be flavored not only with vegetables, but also with the interpretation you bring to it, right?

That is what dreams are like. You collect various expressions, emotions, and events that you use in your life as if you were buying vegetables from the market, and then you cook. What you see in your dreams is a reflection of your experiences. If what you collect with expression, event, and emotion in your daily life consists of potatoes, leeks, onions, and carrots, then in your dream you cook a leek dish. The taste of the dream is determined by what you will contribute to it from your soul. From this point on, you can identify yourself by what is conveyed through symbolic language into your soul and being.

You can take guidance from your dreams. No dream is seen in vain. There is no meaninglessness or nonsense in dreams because every expression is a letter of a state reflected from you in the order of the universe. However, when you do not read this letter transferred to you correctly, what you see may seem nonsense. When you show a baby a very valuable book, the baby will naturally be interested in the color of the book, not its content. The book in the baby's hand is just a red-colored object. The only thing it can perceive is color. Only when the baby grows up and learns how to read and write, can he be interested and able to understand the content of the book.

Every object and every symbol you see in your dreams are each actually a letter placed in the dream.

Let's say you saw an old temple or a madrasa in your dream. This symbol is related to an old reality of yours. In other words, it is a place related to an understanding you have established with it.

Some dream interpreters categorize symbols. For example, they put forward a generic and precise interpretation such as "To see a dog in a dream is hostility". However, the dog is only a letter in a dream and it is not logical to attribute only one meaning to this letter. The color of the dog, its size, who it is with, where it stands, how it makes the dreamer feel, and its connection with the other letters in the dream completely alter the interpretation of the dream.

Interpreting dreams without establishing these connections would be an incomplete interpretation. Although the dream is our way of interpreting life, it is an entirely different art to make an evaluation by bringing together the symbols in the dream.

The better you learn the symbolic language of dreams, the better you will understand and analyze the transmitted information.

Reading the language of events and reading the language of dreams are similar to one another.

At this point, let's also mention simple concepts about dreams:

*If you are dreaming of flat energy, that is, someone is in a reclining position, or you are seeing a cat, or you are dreaming of a woman, a girl, or you are in the dark; all these are about memories, traces from the past, or material issues. These symbols, which are items of the female principle, also indicate the body.

If you are seeing symbols on the move, or if you see a boy, father, or man, you are receiving a message from a dream that indicates issues related to your future. Vertical shapes, which are items of the masculine principle, being on a climb and rising also tell about what will happen in the future and inspirations.

*Each color and symbol in the dream tells something different.

*All the places in the dream tell you the areas where you position yourself, the subjects of the feminine principle, and the reflection of what is happening in life upon you. Let's say you saw that you were in an apartment building. You are in the elevator, there is a man from the office next to you, and the elevator begins to fall rapidly. This dream indicates that you are afraid of falling fast in business or losing your job.

Awareness awakens you from life dreams, event dreams, and spiritual dreams.

Dreams are one of the states that tell and convey you to you, just like the event mirror. However, if you do not fully comprehend it, you may have trouble interpreting it. Still, it is important to record your dreams so that it is easier for you to remember them. The more you learn the language of dreams, the easier it is to interpret them.

The people you see in your dreams also convey their messages with the language of symbols. When you dream of a friend, before calling them and saying, "You know, I dreamed of you, you were doing such and such," you should remember that the dream firstly sends a message to the person who sees it. Then comes the interpretation of the connection with the person you see. In other words, what we see in dreams tells us about us. The friend, or the water, or the sea in the dream are actually what was conveyed to you for you. Just like the events you experience... Because the expressions, events and accidents in life are also meant to tell you about you.

Of course, there are those who do not remember their dreams. These are usually the ones who have somewhat reduced their connection to their soul a little. They ignore what is conveyed from their essence. When they really start to hear and listen, the dream door will reopen for them. Dreams are an important area of guidance.

In short, all dreams are fax messages you send to your soul and essence. "This is my state, I ate and drank these during the day, what is my state?" These are the messages you send and to which you wait for the answer. You also interpret with your soul the state of your spiritual life through your dreams. That is why, it is really important that dreams are not only read but also noticed.

PART II

THE GUIDANCE OF MIND

It is Possible to Program the Brain Correctly by Feeding the Soul

Have you ever thought about how you walk down stairs? How can you do this while rapidly descending the steps? How do you give this command to your body?

The brain develops some systems with the codes it receives and performs some movements automatically. Thanks to the system called "automatism," we do not need to learn the same things time and again. For automatically performed actions such as climbing stairs, eating, learning the address you live in, meeting daily bodily needs, the brain records repetitive actions in order not to exert effort as if learning everything anew each time. This automation system is one of the ways our brains develop to add advantages to our lives. It is a system of adapting to life strongly.

But what happens when this coding and habituation process goes to the extreme? That is when 'robotization' begins. As in primitive thought systems in which awareness and consciousness were low, the brain begins to be coded only with the motives of nutrition, sexuality, and survival. Now, there is only survival and pleasure for the brain. A brain with such a nature can be easily coded and manipulated from the outside because its expectations from life is limited. It exists in order to survive and to enjoy... It becomes easier to manage the brain with expectations. People who are easily manipulated can be coded with the frequencies of certain images, TV series, movies, information, or belief patterns with various sounds and repetitive frequencies. They can also be programmed with some hypnotic words and phrases. It is even possible to code brains with such nature with therapies carried out under the name of 'mind programming systems.'

In short, the brain is both trainable and manageable. What matters is who controls the brain... Will you manage your brain or will you be managed from outside?

My word is to those who want to rule themselves...

If you want to purify your brain from coding with data that you unknowingly take from outside, which creates a desire in you to do things of which you are disturbed by the results in some aspects, then you must first get away from living a life focused on pleasure, from your routines and your addictions because the point from which you have been captured is your weakness and you will continue to be ruled from there.

For example, let's look at some behavioral patterns that you exhibit every day and cannot stop yourself from doing: watching TV, spending time on the Internet, drinking coffee, etc...

For whatever you say, "I can't come to myself without doing it," has become a routine and behavior that has been ruling over you. Even if you think that these behaviors are serving you, you are actually serving them. A servant does what they are told. The word of the one receiving the service prevails. If it says, "Drink me," you drink it. The power of which you follow the command is your boss now.

Look at what/who you are giving the power.

Cigarette

Alcohol

Drug

TV

Phone

Internet

Lover

Sweet

Coffee

Surely, the list can go on...

Of course, in every era and every order, there will the ones who stay at the bottom and those who ascend. Those who ascend are the ones who are lively and use their minds, who act with their heart, and not with the herd.

Listen; the more you listen, the more you are listened to.
Watch; you learn about yourself from what you are watching...

How to feed the brain in order to gravitate towards the truth? Observe if you repeat the same things every day. Do you always eat the same food? Do you watch the same series, do you always wear the same clothes in the same style, do you spend your life with the system you are used to, do you always have the same point of view?

In that case, you are restricting yourself to a narrow view, a narrow belief pattern, by limiting yourself with such a thought: "The possibilities that life offers me are certain, what I can do is limited, I am already doing the best I can and I am living my life one way or another."

New experiences support us to meet the new. If you want to invite new things into your life, turn to new things in your diet, expressions, and actions.

What has happened is the best of what has happened
and will happen.

PART III

READING THE CHOICES

Your profession choses you

Do you own a job or does your job own you?
No...

I'm not talking about whether you are your own boss or not. I focus on your work. Who sits in your executive chair? Do your business principles or status rule you, or are they just your signature?

You often think you have to get a job to earn money or status, right? It is likely that you are not fully paid for your work. But whenever working and producing become your signature to life, then your earnings are blessed and your work becomes a tool that helps you savor life.

If you describe yourself as someone's spouse, child, the manager or owner, employee, or president of a company, it means that you are trying to build your identity in order to prove yourself to others. In this case, the meaning of life will surely move away from you. Most people use their position, money, and status to gain superiority over others.

Their aim is to show themselves off because they overly beat themselves up for everything that they achieve. This attitude first affects the body and then mental and spiritual health. Another of the lost values is time here.

A wise person once said that people lose their health working a life time to make money and then spend their money to regain their health.

If your profession serves your purpose in life and if you can live with your earnings, then your identity represents you.

Let's do some reading on professions together, shall we?

Teachers: their learning capacity and persuasion abilities have developed. They need to develop themselves more in whatever field their teaching ability has developed. Therefore, they tell the same information in different ways. They feel the need to teach because they feel the need to learn.

"What I tell best is what I need most."

Screenwriters: they have a rich imagination. They need to realize the fiction of the flow in their own life. They hardly use their imagination for their own life. When they start to use this treasure for themselves, their life becomes delicious.

Actors: thanks to their intuitive and visual observation skills, they have a high ability to empathize. As a result of the roles they take on throughout their career, they can gain experience as if they have lived many lives.

When they use their power to understand others in order to understand themselves, they can notice the pressure they feel on themselves, thus unleash themselves from it.

Physicians: Their ability to identify problems and make connections, as well as their power of external observation are quite high. They can focus on solving problems. That's why, they find it difficult to let things slide. It helps them to get help from others when they have a problem, just the way they can solve other people's problems.

Lawyers: they have a high understanding of equity, justice, and grace. They have the potential to leave their own emotional and physical areas vulnerable. They may also have the potential to carry the struggle for rightfulness to defend others to all facets of life. This may force them to remain neutral. It can be good for them to listen, especially to do deep listening practice.

Judges: their ability of deep listening and intuitiveness is high. Their sense of justice and equity is developed. They may have difficulty in being a decision-maker in life. They need to make choices for their own benefit in their own life.

Writers: their ability to write or explain a topic is good. They may have difficulty explaining themselves to others as well as to themselves. Stagnation is not good for the writer. Stimulating areas create vivacity.

Psychologists: they listen well, make observations, and have a strong ability to draw conclusions from events. They focus on cause-effect relations. Since they are focused on detecting certain situations in others, they may hesitate to focus on their own lives and to be sure of the steps they take. It is good for them to look at themselves and their life plan objectively.

Accountants: They have the ability to see such minor nuances of an event that can be overlooked. Their ability to sort out is strong. They may have trouble distinguishing between what is useful and what is useless in their own life. It helps them to be able to look at events and the course of their life from a wider perspective.

Historians, Archeologists, Anthropologists: They have a good memory, as well as the ability to comprehend and analyze well. Their visual memory is developed. They choose this profession in order to discover the situations and states inherited from ancestors and transform the legacy of the past in themselves. They need to be freed from the past and recurring events.

Those who work as a health, food, or service provider to others: They are good at understanding what someone else needs. Their social intelligence is high. They have the ability to detect and solve problems. Since they do not know what changes to make in their lives, they have difficulty in change. They may experience recurrent events. It helps them to identify their own needs and prioritize themselves.

Drivers: They are good at focusing on a goal, coordinating, and finding solutions. They may find it difficult to innovate in their own lives and set goals for advancement. What they need is to let go of repetition and abandon the routine.

Those working in construction: They are planners in putting the pieces together and taking steps towards the future. They find it difficult to maintain integrity in their own lives. They live fast in one period and stagnant in another. They need stability. Being consistent in their family and social relations will support them.

Your work at a specific period and at a specific job indicates that you have chosen that profession for the subjects you need to complete and learn in that field. Your profession, too, has come to you completely according to your demand in order to meet a need of yours. Reading by watching yourself and those around you from this perspective will contribute significantly to you and your relationships.

Reading Relationships

A woman's husband represents her current future plans, her spirituality, and her approach to the divine system. A man's wife represents his view of material and worldly affairs, as well as his view of the past.

The strength of a man's economy is influenced by his interactions with women. His attitude towards women actually shows his approach to his material world. Those who cannot catch the rhythm they seek in business life are usually tense with one of the women in their family; either with their mother, wife, or with an issue they experienced in the past.

If the male role model of the house is going out of town to work, the decision-making mechanism in the family is passed to the woman. Although the problem here seems to be resolved from the outside, in fact, women often send their men away when they cannot easily accept to receive from the masculine principle. If a woman complains about her boyfriend or husband, she has many issues to which she objects in life; she does not find life fair; the problems she experienced with her father in the past prevent her from trusting the men in her life.

If a man wants to be successful, he must be respectful, loving, and loyal to his woman. If a man is cheating on his wife, he is cheating himself about financial matters, i.e., he works money-oriented or he is overconfident in financial power. There are people deceiving him with his job, with his body, or in any other area of life.

If a woman wants to trust her future, live life with its flow, and be at peace with her inner voice, she should be respectful, full of love, and loyal to her man. If a woman continues to be together with a man while complaining about him, this is also cheating. She is deceiving herself first and then her spiritual plan. In this case, she cannot look at her future with confidence, she cannot listen to the voice of her heart. If a woman wants to walk on her spiritual plan by feeding on her inspirations, and if she has a relationship that is not going well, she will have to either fix it or stop complaining, end the relationship and find peace.

When a woman or a man feels peaceful and happy, they reflect this to their partners and nurtures them. You will not get anywhere by just focusing on making the other person happy and acting accordingly. This attitude is the desire to change the other person's perspective about you. Remember that it is you who is reflected in the mirror.

As long as the man treats his wife as if she is his mother, and the wife treats her husband as if he is her father, it is difficult for them to find harmony. There is no coming from the old family to the new one.

If an emotional relationship cannot start in a woman's or man's life, there may be something they do not want to break in their relationship with their parents, or the emotional bond and influence of a finished relationship still continue.

In any case, in order to heal and wake up, make your ears hear what you say, so that you can change your situation with your intention.

Locations Speak

Not only our expressions, choices, repetitions, professions, but naturally our places also express us, reflect us. Our workplaces, homes, study rooms, summer houses, places we prefer to have fun... Every place we are in, even the clothes we wear tell a lot about us when we want to read and understand them.

Every system in the established order is transferred to us as a mirror of our energies. For example, observe where you live; do you see a pointed object pointing at you?

Think of these as arrows pointing at you; you may be feeling threatened. Upward pointed shapes indicate your attempt to raise the energy, while downward pointed shapes indicate the desire to bring the energy down.

Look at the details you like or dislike about your location. Is it messy or orderly? If you are messy, you may struggle to finish the things you start and make plans for the future, or maybe you are not able to put them into practice.

Are there any broken items around? Look for the reason you keep the broken items, do you have an emotional connection with them, do you think you cannot get new ones? You may be a controlling person, or you may have trouble letting go.

Are your paid or unpaid bills somewhere around? The ones you keep in the sight are the ones that occupy your mind the most.

Where are your family photos and what age period do they belong to? Finding out why you chose these photos will provide you with insight. Examine your drawers, too... The stuff accumulated in the storage areas will make it easier for you to remember and analyze. I suggest you also check the glove compartment of the car. Open it up and see what you find.

Burned out light bulbs in the house, blisters on walls, broken surfaces, stained carpets... The fact that the meaningless stored items are still there even though they are no longer needed and have lost their function, actually speaks of your experiences that you cannot leave behind.

One of my consultees had clogged toilets both at work and at home. Even though plumbers came and fixed them, the same problem reoccurred.

"What do you think this situation is telling me?" she asked me. I told her, "There may be things that you have difficulty in quitting and therefore cannot move forward to your future, so you are stuck with those things."

Afterwards, we saw that even though she broke up with her husband years ago, she could not break the internal emotional bond with him. Her ex, whom she could not leave, was preventing her from getting a new boyfriend in her life. Realizing that the ties she could not break with her ex were harming her and hindering her progress, she decided to cut them. Clogged toilets signaled to her a blockage in her life. While the toilets were being repaired, she focused on what happened, did not dismiss the reason, and began to question. This questioning led her to an issue she could not solve emotionally and untied a knot she was unaware of.

The old building next to the house of a friend of mine had been demolished due to urban transformation. There was constant construction noise from outside and my friend was very tense because of how long this work was taking. He was very disturbed by the noise.

I told him what this construction meant. I said that an old reality was being destroyed and would be rebuilt. As soon as he realized in which areas this was a renewal, he moved to another district because now the need to watch that construction was over. When he focused on the main message of the event, which he perceived as discomfort rather than construction, he established a unity between himself and life.

One day, a mother who said that her family had suffered severe accidents and that she had some problems asked me for help. The sharp corner of the high-rise building directly opposite her house intersected exactly with the living room of her house. Living rooms symbolize social life. Ever since they moved into this house, they have been experiencing disturbing incidents and attacks on social media. Their social life was quite tiring and they realized that they could not spare time for each other as a family. They reduced their posts on social media. Then, we placed an object in the living room that would embrace and reduce the physical effect of the pointed shape opposite the house, and thus we bent its energy. Most importantly, my consultee realized that she had not attached much importance to family unity in the face of the problems she was experiencing. Thus, she changed her areas of focus and started to care about family privacy and the problems solved themselves.

The direction the desk faces in the workplace also gives an important message. Let's say you work at a desk next to the toilet. You are in a smelly place where everyone leaves their trash, or you are opposite the door... If you pay attention to why you are sitting at this desk before changing its position, you may realize that you take a load from others, that you may make comments about their past, and that these comments negatively affect your life. Now, with your awakening in your mind, you have already put a distance between you and that trash, door, or problem. The physical solution you need for the position of the desk will come by itself, or you can take a step towards a solution by placing an object between you and that energy.

Places also reflect what is in you,
just like your verbal expressions, behaviors, and choices.
It is not a notion outside or beyond you.
They are intermediaries that point to what is in you.
Every item, every object, every color --from its size to its
position—is a reflection of an expression about you.
Just like your verbal expressions, the locations you use or you are
in reflect what is in you.

Still water: It is necessary to be careful and pay attention to still water because water has a stopping energy, too. It may be that something flowing in your life has been stopped. There may be stagnation in the flow of money, information, spiritual matters, love, affection, and sexuality. It is important to be aware of the still water in an inoperative aquarium, pond, or vase. Keeping still water at home is like a stagnation spell by your own hand. Still water signifies the cessation of creativity, feminine energy, and productivity.

In location readings,
we realize what we have been doing to our own lives.
Now we have created with objects what
we have created with expressions.
We have unwittingly chosen the objects
that will lead to a knot or solution in our fate.

Stopped watch/clock: Using time in the wrong places, wasting it, or not making progress because of an issue in which you are stuck. The desire to stop something.

Broken china: Your inability to withdraw from areas where you think you were hurt or harmed in the past.

Family photos: The desire to be or to continue with the family, the desire to repeat the past, and the reluctance to renew yourself.

Paintings and photos: Chaos, rough sea, unhappy people, ruined buildings, mythological symbols the meanings of which you do not know, paintings or photographs with weapons and war attract the energies they contain into your life. The fact that you have chosen and used these means that you have a conflict within yourself, that you need to drag your life down, and that you need things to go in a direction you do not want. The objects you use should be motivating.

Library: Relying on knowledge and what you know, continuing what you know...

Pointed objects: It collects the energy at one point and channels it wherever its direction is like an arrow. If it is up, it raises the energy; if it is down, it lowers the energy. It would be wise to use chandeliers carefully, especially in bedrooms.

Oval stuff: It softens, calms, and facilitates the flow of energy. You can use globe-shaped lamps, spherical and egg-shaped natural stones.

White: You invite death to the area and energy field in a room where you go to extremes in the use of white. White symbolizes death as well as enlightenment, and rebirth. Therefore, with its radiant effect, it can give satisfactory results in places where new ideas, creativity, and the implementation of rules are desired, as well as in clinics and hospitals to symbolize the death of diseases and physical ailments, thus the rebirth of health. The color white also symbolizes authority.

Red: It symbolizes fire and mobility. It starts and ends things. Using the color red intensely in a space can both increase and stop the movement. It is best to be in balance.

Yellow: Using yellow intensely at home is the desire to be extremely strong and controlling. Intense control mostly overwhelms. Controllessness increases in your life. You will experience a lot of difficulties that you cannot oversee and that get out of control because what you want is power. Those who ask for power will be given power. Those who have difficulties in their lives are those who want to have power the most. Surely, there is need to go through difficulties to get strong. The system duly meets your request all the time.

Black: The reason for the intense use of the color black at home is the need for protection. If the need for protection is directed to black with the feeling of fear and if the dominant color of the house is black, this choice leads to darkness. However, using a sufficient amount of black is protective. It is important for black to be balanced.

Green: Places with the color green in the house give calmness. It carries the energy of freshness, vitality and birth. Using it in a balanced way feeds the energy of movement whereas its heavy use can slow down the movement.

Now, let's see in what kind of neighborhood and location your house is, since you have chosen everything according to your needs, from the street you are on to the door number of the apartment you live in, and none of this is a coincidence...

The kind of neighborhood, the characteristics of the street you live on and even the name of the apartment you live in are important information used in location readings. You have not chosen your location in vain. What matters is not to change the neighborhood or house you live in, but to find out and understand why you have chosen it in the first place. By correctly reading the place you live in, you can easily receive the message that the whole conveys to you.

If the door or window of your house overlooks the garbage, there are things in your past that you cannot let go of. Smelling the stench of garbage shows how much the things you could not let go of are bothering you today.

If the door or window of your house views a pleasant green area, you are open to renewal. If the door or window of the house is facing other buildings, you cannot see the horizon very well. If it is facing the pool, water can bring abundance and wealth.

You can also provide these types of energies with the paintings, pictures, or quilts you use at home. You can bend energy without moving house. You can liberate both yourself and your future by realizing why and what you have experienced or have not been able to experience until now.

PART IV

THE RHYTYM AND FLOW OF LIFE

Read Your Body through the Flow of Nature

Nature has a rhythm and flow. The cycle that continues within the ecological system operates with a mechanism that both feeds and is fed on by each other. Death makes room for newborns. Plants feed herbivores, herbivores feed carnivores, carnivores die and feed what is in the soil, and the soil turns green again. This mechanism is like a heartbeat, allocating resources, collecting waste, cleaning, and redistributing.

From the moment we disrupt this rhythm and begin to interpret it according to ourselves, our body rhythm begins to deteriorate and we contract diseases. It is argued that the first diseases were transmitted by animals living next to settled humans. Until the industrial revolution, the biggest problem was seeking cures and treating diseases and complications caused by injuries. Prior to Western medicine, medical practice was mostly based on diagnosing by reading the patient's body. Focusing on finding the cause of the disrupted rhythm, the physician would restore the patient to health with hunger, herbal solutions, and baths. While the basic principles in Western medicine were based on monitoring bodily symptoms, it later turned to reading data from analytical devices. In a short span of one century, the systems that were supported by nature for thousands of years were left behind. The emphasis has shifted to the use of chemicals.

Germany and England, which have been considered as rapidly mechanized countries where modern medicine was born, have recently turned to traditional methods in health systems. The practice of not only herbal therapies, but also holistic health approaches has increased considerably to prevent the problem from occurring.

I discovered over time that the Far-Eastern approaches to health, which I came across thanks to judo that I started at the age of ten, were also used by the Uyghur Turks. I also had the opportunity to examine the works written by İbn-i Sina, İbn-i Baytar, and İbn-i Şerif. Over time, I have made use of this information to read life and to preserve the health of the body. The information I will share with you here is the basic principles that you can use in body, emotion, and location readings. When we live with the flow of nature, we are supported by the system we are in. This flow also has a language. Once you learn the cycle, it becomes easier for you to read and interpret your body, your emotional fluctuations, and the possible consequences of events. In ancient sources, the factors of the natural cycle were defined as elements, which support and bring into existence each other in a natural flow. When they work adversely, they destroy the existing ones and cause diseases. There are also those that block each other's flow.

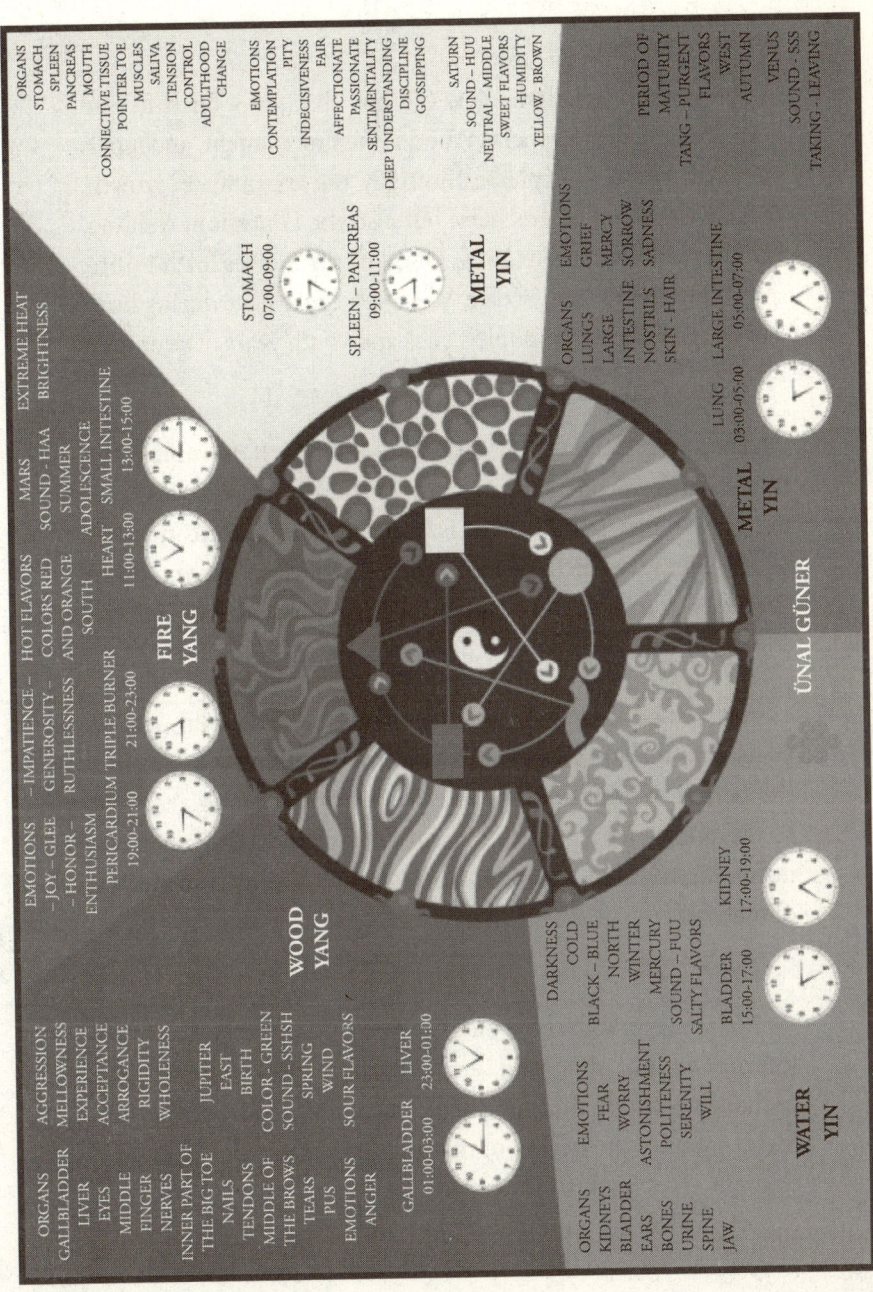

Constructive Cycle

In this cycle, each element is the one that gives birth to and nourishes the next element. Wood is the first element, and it tells our birth phase. It expresses not only the appearance, growth, and development of greenery, but also the education, training, and development in our lives. Wood element gives birth to fire, so you progress as you evolve. What you experience during birth and infancy affects the adolescence and youth years of your life.

Wood ⇄ Fire

The fire element symbolizes moving. It signifies the transition from one state to another, the joy of progress. It is the growth phase of life; that is, the phases of adolescence and youth. Fire gives birth to earth from its ashes. What you do in the years of your youth affects your period of maturity.

Fire ⇄ Earth

Soil symbolizes being able to reveal one's potential, setting goals, and realizing long-term plans by accepting what is. It is the period of adulthood in life. The earth element gives birth to the metal element with what it adds from itself. What you do in adulthood determines how you will live in your period of maturity.

Earth ⇄ Metal

Metal symbolizes being able to make decisions, internalization, digesting experiences, and realizing the exchange with life through the power it absorbs from the soil. Metal signifies the period of maturity in human life. The metal element gives birth to water with its own additives. What you experience during your maturity period determines the rhythm of your old age and the brew you have taken from life.

Metal ⇄ Water

The water element is the state you have reached based on the conclusions you have drawn from what you have experienced in your entire life. It is the period of expressing satisfaction or complaints from all that has happened. It symbolizes the old age period of human life and the termination of life. The water element is the field where the transition from one state to another will be experienced.

You need to remember that an illness you have, things that you cannot overcome emotionally, and the part that goes to the extreme in order to track the problems you have in relationships will affect the whole cycle.

When there is a problem with the earth element, the metal becomes problematic, then it affects the water element. Water cannot feed the tree, the fire weakens and so the earth weakens. In other words, the system that has deteriorated in the soil cycles back and hits the soil again. To break this cycle, it is necessary to strengthen the water and the tree. The tree nourished with water nourishes the fire and the earth becomes stronger.

The cause of your stomach problem is related to your liver and your anger towards what you have experienced in the past. The acid rate in the stomach might have increased and an ulcer may have formed. You can look at your relationship with liquid nutrients to heal your stomach.

In order to heal the liver, you should have an alkaline diet and eat fresh and green vegetables. This also strengthens the kidneys. There is also a destructive counterpart of this constructive cycle. In the constructive cycle, each element gives birth to and nourishes the next element. However, in the destructive and controlling cycle, each element attacks the following two elements, and either weakens or limits them.

Destructive Cycle

Wood ⇆ Earth

When the wood element goes to extremes, so does the fire and it gets out of control, thus cannot adequately feed the earth element it will give birth to, and the earth is damaged. Problems in birth and infancy, exuberance during adolescence can lead to going to extremes. This may have undesirable consequences in adulthood. The earth element symbolizes the stomach, spleen, pancreas, and muscles in the body. The emotional cause of the problems that occur here is the anger with what has happened and not being able to be flexible towards events.

Fire ⇆ Metal

When the fire element goes to extremes, first the earth and then the metal element will be damaged. Since fire cannot adequately feed the earth, weak earth gives birth to weak metal. Excessive fatigue and wrong choices in nutrition in youth can cause large intestine and lung problems in maturity. The causes of problems in the large intestine are anemia, problems in stomach digestion, malfunction of the spleen, incapacity of the pancreas in regulating the sugar in the blood. Behind all this, there is sadness in the emotion, lack of joy, errors in nutrition that affect the small intestine, and imbalances that affect the blood rhythm.

Earth ⇆ Water

When the earth element goes to extremes; that is, when it loses its balance, the metal weakens and the water is damaged. Those who do not have long-term plans in adulthood, those who live day-to-day, those who want events to go according to their own will and feed on tension, those who are used to stress experience problems in their kidneys, genital organs, and bones in old age. They also become anxious, insecure about themselves and life because of their decisions.

When you cannot accept and digest as an experience what you have gone through in your years of maturity, you cannot leave your memories in the past, and therefore your fear of losing increases.

Water ⇄ Fire

When the water element goes to extremes, the tree is weakened and the fire is damaged. Not being able to leave past experiences behind and not being able to let events flow create a feeling of having lost ground. Not being able to know where you belong and why you are living this life extinguishes the fire of life. What is accumulated in the body over the years pollutes the blood and reduces the fire. So, the whole system is affected by heart fatigue, heart diseases, and circulatory problems. The basic emotion here is the lack of joy.

The strength and well-being of one element enrich and nourish the next. It balances the next one with a beneficial control system. You can use these principles in all the cycles of nature, body, and life.

What Do Elements Tell Us in General?

Wood Element: It represents the birth of nature, humans and living things. Its direction is east, its taste is sour, and its color is green. Its internal organs are the liver and gallbladder. Its facial organ is the eye. Its place in the body is the nervous system, tendons, and nails. Its fluids in the body are tears and pus. Its positive emotions are mellowness and experience. Its negative emotions are anger, irritability, rigidity, and arrogance.

Fire Element: It represents childhood and adolescence in life. Its direction is south, its taste is hot/bitter and its color is red. It is the element of heat and summer. Its internal organs are the heart and small intestine. The facial organ is the tongue. Its place in the body is the circulatory system and the pericardium. Its fluid in the body is sweat. Its positive emotions are joy, glee, honor, and enthusiasm. Its negative emotions are impatience, cruelty, and extravagance.

Earth Element: It corresponds to the period of adulthood in life. Its direction is central, its taste is sweet, its color is yellow. It is the element of the end of summer, and the neutral. Its internal organs are the stomach, spleen, and pancreas. Its facial organ is the mouth. Its representations in the body are muscles and connective tissues. Its fluid is saliva. Its positive emotions are experience, contemplation, determination, fairness, and control. Its negative emotions are tension, control, pity, indecision, gossip, sentimentalism, and tearfulness.

Metal Element: It represents autumn, the period of maturity and coolness. Its color is white and gray. Its internal organs are the lungs and large intestine. Its facial organ is the nose. Its representation in the body is the skin. Its direction is west. Its positive emotions are compassion and forgiveness. Its negative emotions are grief, sadness, and sorrow. It is the symbol of the ability to receive and let go. Its flavors are bitter and pungent ones.

Water Element: It represents the season of winter, the cold, dark, and black. Its direction is north, its taste is salty. Its internal organs are the kidney and bladder. Its facial organ is the ears. Its fluid is urine. It is represented by the bone and spinal cord in the bodily system. It carries the properties and energy of water.

Every element in our body is defined as either masculine or feminine. Organs working with the feminine principle are the heart, kidneys, spleen, lung, and liver. Organs working with the masculine principle are the stomach, gallbladder, large intestines, small intestines, and bladder.

Masculine organs represent the future and plans for the future, the relationship with the father, the inheritance of feelings and behavior transmitted from the father, relations with men, spiritual sensations, and authority figures. Their positive emotions are to set free, to feel safe, and to have courage. Their negative emotions and behaviors are insecurity and a desire to control due to insecurity, aggression caused by fear, arrogance, rigidity, and ruthlessness.

The feminine organs represent the projection of the past to the present, the behavioral patterns acquired in the past, the emotional bond with women, the mother, body, material notions, and the living space. Their positive emotions and behaviors are to accept what has been experienced with love, to feel being approved, to be able to feed on life, to be soft, flexible, and tolerant. Their negative emotions and behaviors are not being able to feel love, lack of joy, sadness, sorrow, grief, panic caused by anxiety, and angry behaviors.

These two principles are also known as giving and receiving. While doing a reading, if the matter is to not be able to receive, we can say that it is about the female principle. If the issue is to not be able to let go, it is about the masculine principle.

For example, we understand that those who have respiratory ailments in their lungs cannot accept and embrace a problem they have with their mother; if it is not about their mother, they have problems to solve with the world. Those who have problems with their bowels, on the other hand, have problems with their father, with authority, and with not being able to quit yet. The body uses these two systems together in every element and provides integrity. Each system has a mother and a father or an organ working with one masculine and one feminine principle.

Wood Element – Liver feminine, gallbladder masculine
Fire Element – Heart feminine, small intestine masculine
Earth Element – Spleen feminine, stomach masculine
Metal Element – Lung feminine, large intestine masculine

When it comes to the brain, it functions just the opposite. The right lobe is feminine, and the left lobe belongs to the masculine principle.

The nervous system is masculine; blood vessels are feminine; the shaped elements of the blood are masculine; and liquid component of the blood is feminine.

In the masculine and feminine organ system, the organs outside the body bending inward, the holes, and the moist ones are feminine. Outward and pointed-shaped organs are masculine.

MASCULINE organs on the outside of the body are the nose, the penis, the eyes, lips and the skin.

FEMININE organs on the outside of the body are the nostrils, ears, the mouth and the vagina.

Let's say the nose, which is representative of the metal element on the face, started to run. This is not just about the nose. It also concerns the lungs and the intestines, which are the other members of the metal element. The condition that you take lightly by calling it a cold also affects your lungs in the future. Therefore, in order to accelerate recovery, the intestines should be emptied and solid food consumption should be given a rest for a while. It is the earth element that gives birth to metal. If the earth, the stomach, is not too tired, the metal will become stronger. If the intestine, which is one of the elements of the metal element, is rested, the lung will gather its strength faster. A cold that starts with a runny nose is about feeling weak and insecure in the face of an unacceptable situation. The immune system is responsible for the body's defense. If the defense was weak, you also felt weak in the face of what you went through. As well as regulating your diet to support your body, taking a compassionate approach to yourself by noticing what you are going through emotionally will help you identify what you need to regain your strength and move away from disease-causing elements before they settle in your lungs and throat. A cold that causes not only a runny nose but also affects the throat indicates that the emotional effect continues. "You are angry that you haven't been able to express yourself." The throat area is associated with expressing. An inflammation/pus formed there indicates that the issue has also spread to the tree element. Now you start to feel sad and insecure and angry about not being able to express yourself adequately.

All inflammations/pus originate from the liver. After the wood element comes into play, the issue is reflected in the nervous system as well. If you cannot solve the problem here, the inflammation/pus goes to the lungs and settles there. What you experience evolves from a minor runny nose to a chronic problem, and the balance of the body becomes impaired. When one element fails, all are affected. Fire is also affected by a deterioration in the wood element, and the fire element rises. If the body does not receive sufficient support from the water system early on, then the disease takes over the body. What we have told so far is a technical explanation.

As to the emotional aspect of this situation: a state that could lead to illness has occurred due to a simple event that has affected you emotionally. Not only diseases that are described as chronic, but also the ones that suddenly appear and the symptoms of which may not have been felt much can be cured even before it starts if the body is well monitored. This awareness can be formed both by establishing physical balance and through comprehension understanding. The realm of matter and spirit is a whole.

Examples about Water and Tree Elements

Bones, joints, blood fluid, kidneys, bladder, liver, gallbladder...

Water is one of the body's main sources of nutrition. Lack of water triggers many ailments in the body. If you do not remember to drink water during the day, if you drink it as an obligation or if you quench your thirst with other liquids other than water, it means that you cannot get something new in your life, you cannot be refreshed. If this situation continues for a long time, it is possible to develop blood fluid density, disorders in the kidneys, and diseases in the bones and the urinary tract. When you remove salt –which is the taste of the water element– from your life, or use refined salt, your state of panic in the face of anxiety and events may increase. When the body cannot reach the source it needs, it finds ways to satisfy its needs with what is available. Since water is the continuity of oxygen and life, cells cannot meet their needs and they start to dry up, almost becoming deserts. This situation, which is the trigger of many diseases, is a result of your resistance to the new, your fear of change, and your desire to continue what is. Even though you are unhappy, your effort to forcefully maintain your relationship in order to keep the family together will not make anyone happy.

Fears can lead people to drink little water. Drinking little water also causes drying and desertification in the cells, while intensifying the fattening between the waist and hips. The result is the same when people drink too much water; and when minerals and salt are not used. When both sides of the scale are in balance, it is possible to behave correctly without learning the right information. You accept innovation, change, transition to an unfamiliar area, take the right amount of water, use natural salt and feel safe.

The brain and spinal cord are also included in the water element. Fear and anxiety, the negative emotion of the water element, are the main cause of brain disorders. Approaching life with confidence and love helps to heal disorders in the brain.

The emotional cause of bones and spine disorders is that you do not have a foundation where you think you belong in life, that you do not have enough resources, that you cannot make your own way, that you cannot build your own building. You have a problem with the skeletal structure you have built in your life. If your spine problem has turned into a herniated disc and the problem is on the right side, it means that you believe that you carry a heavy load for your future, and if the problem is on the left side, you carry more than you can handle regarding financial matters.

If there is pain, strain, or noises during movement in the knee joints, there is an accumulation of acid in your body. There has been a shift from alkali to acid in the synovial fluid, the body's most alkaline fluid. The real receiver of this message is the gallbladder. Fatigue began in the liver; acidic diet, excessive animal food, frying, and consumption of acidic beverages have created a problem in the wood element. You have not taken enough water into the body in order to clear the traces of this diet, so the residues of body waste damage the joints. If we interpret this emotionally, that means you have not been able to be flexible in life as a result of your resistance to changing what you learn and know, and continued to be rigid and firm when you needed to become more flexible. The inability to kneel to life and the inability to be flexible when facing events surface as a discomfort starting in the knees.

This example clearly puts forth that if you do not drink water, which gives birth to the wood element in the life cycle, you also harm the organs –the liver and gallbladder– of the wood element, too. Those who are resistant to innovation and flexibility will dry out and not lubricate themselves, just as vegetables put into hot oil will dry out and even burn if they stay in the oil a little too long. Therefore, when you cannot take action in the face of a situation, your anger increases, and your increased anger makes you want to consume oily and fried foods. This diet increases your desire to drink acidic, cold, and fizzy drinks instead of drinking water. This means that the cycle becomes destructive.

People who are governed by anger but do not eat acidic or fatty foods, feed on angry people in events, relationships, and the issues they focus on. Most of the people who are calm, who have a healthy diet, and are in harmony with their environment are in a state of anger at those criticizing, judging, and blaming what is happening outside, and exhibiting behaviors that they object to. This is what it means to feed on the anger frequency through events and relationships.

The acid, which is the result of the pollution caused by the diet or negative emotions of the person who chooses to live in the anger frequency, leads to the formation of kidney stones in the kidneys. Those with kidney stones have problems in their stomach and pancreas. Although a kidney stone is a product of the frequency of anger, the source of that anger is the tension and the state of "It should be as I say" created by the desire to control. The person has been drinking little water, eating plenty of solid and acidic food, thus has disturbed the stomach's acid balance.

If you remember, I mentioned that the water element is in charge of all liquids. Although the stomach is a member of the earth element, gastric fluid is related to the water element. The water element represents the end of life. So, you should remember that when you do not drink water, you terminate an energy somewhere in your body. The emotion of the water element is trust. The more you trust life, the more you let go of control and begin to heal.

Examples about Fire and Earth Elements

Heart, small intestine, stomach, pancreas, spleen...

If the wood element is in balance, the fire created by the wood will also be strong and balanced. As long as we remember that each element is interrelated, we would know that the point of origin of the problem is the result, and the source of the problem is the solution.

Especially those who think that they are not loved by their family are more likely to experience heart and small intestine problems. When the story of their birth is being told by the family, those who keep hearing statements such as "We expected you to be a boy" or "a girl" or "you were born at a time when we weren't ready for you. We thought about having an abortion, we seriously considered it" are conditioned to not being approved or loved. This conditioning is the root cause of various blood and heart diseases, especially low blood pressure. The source of the feeling of worthlessness comes from disapproval by the family. The premature death of a family member, a parent leaving the family and/or the child reinforces the belief of worthlessness. This is a factor that reduces the fire of life. When a problem occurs in the element of fire, we see that that person's excitement, the joy of life, and desire to progress in a subject are low. Now, what you need to remember here is that when the fire element is weak, the earth will also be weak. Accordingly, those who have little joy in life and do not feel loved enough will need to constantly check outside because they do not trust life. This may lead to stomach disorders, pancreas, spleen, muscle disorders, and later to large intestine or genital organ diseases.

Water extinguishes the fire, wood feeds it, and the earth weakens it in the body, as in the physics of life.

When you cannot get enough love and joy in life, your side that wants to change the past or complains about it damages your pancreas. The pancreas is such an organ that it is the center of the energy source of all organs and systems in the body. A blockage here can lead to a decrease in the strength of the entire body, life becomes joyless and flavorless. When you listen to someone with diabetes around you, you will realize how much they complain about the past.

The stomach and pancreas, the two organs of the earth element, become unhealthy with control, tension and complaints. Whether it is yourself or others that are complaining, it is actually gossip energy. The energy of gossip creates a cycle of desperation that causes you to feel sorry for yourself, become overly sensitive, and cry a lot. This is a sign that your blood is contaminated. It causes swelling, especially in the joints of the big toe (bunions).

When you stop complaining and criticizing to the extent of gossiping, your body starts to clean the blood. To get support from nature, you can eat yellow-colored foods, great yellow gentian oil for the stomach, balsam apple for the pancreas, antioxidant red and purple vegetables and fruits for the spleen.

The flavors that strengthen the fire element are bitterness and red-colored foods. Fresh green foods and sour flavors nourish the heart.

Examples about Metal Elements

Large intestine, lungs, skin...

In the natural cycle of life, autumn is the season that we consider as preparation for winter. Vegetables and fruits that come out in this season are mostly white in color, have strong tastes, and are rich in pulp. With these foods, the intestines work well and clean themselves. A purified bowel means a strong immune system. While the weather is getting colder, warming flavors protect the body against the coolness of the air and prepare it for winter. When you continue to consume summer vegetables and fruits during this season, the body becomes unable to protect itself due to their cooling effect. You can nourish your intestines and lungs better by strengthening the earth element. In particular, you can eat foods such as potatoes, pumpkin, and bananas, which are slightly sweet and rich in potassium. Relaxing and going with the flow makes both the stomach and the large intestine comfortable. The lungs, the other member of the metal element, are easily affected by the positive or negative activity in the large intestine. When the intestines cannot empty, the lungs become more susceptible to colds. Therefore, it is important to ensure the discharge of the large intestine at the beginning of the common cold. Thus, the immune system is activated more easily.

If letting go is a difficult action for you, you are likely to experience discomforts such as constipation, colitis, and hemorrhoids. When you have a problem with your large intestines or lungs, you should remember that the triggering factor is heartbreak, deep sorrow, or an emotional distress that cannot be left behind.

Diseases that occur on the skin, which is the representative of this element in the senses, are caused by feeling unprotected, vulnerable and anxious against harm that may come from outside. Allergies are mostly caused by the metal element and the emotions it represents. You can easily detect from the retina of your eyes whether there is a problem with the metal element in your body. The redness and bleeding in the white part of your eyes are related to your large intestines and the emotions you cannot digest. The redness in the white part towards the outer corners of your eyes is related to your lungs and not being able to accept what you are going through.

ELEMENT	ORGAN AND SYSTEM	DISEASE	EMOTION	EXPRESSIONS HERALDING THE ISSUE	SYSTEMS NEEDING SUPPORT TO HEAL
WOOD	LIVER, GALLBLADDER, NERVOUS SYSTEM, EYES	DISEASES RELATED TO THE LIVER, EYES, AND NERVOUS SYSTEM; PUS; ACHNES; STIFFNESSES; DISORDERS RELATED TO WEIGHT AND LUBRICATION IN THE VEINS; GALLBLADDER ISSUES; SYNAPSES; TENDONS; PHYSICAL POWER SOURCE; FAT METABOLISM; CELLULITE; TICS	ANGER, AGGRESSION, RAGE, ARROGANCE, FEELING OF WORTHLESSNESS	DEFINITELY, NEVER, NO WAY, ABSOLUTELY NOT; YOW, PISH, "ONLY I KNOW THIS!"	WATER SYSTEM, DRINKING WATER, BALANCE OF MINERALS, CORRECT USE OF SALT, BALANCING ACID AND ALKALINE, SOUR FLAVORS, ALKALI FOODS, INCREASING THE CONSUMPTION OF GREEN AND RAW VEGETABLES, USE OF THE COLOR GREEN
FIRE	HEART, SMALL INTESTINE, BLOOD VESSELS, BLOOD CIRCULATION, TONGUE, PERICARDIUM, TRIPLE BURNER, BLOOD	HEART DISEASES, VASCULAR PROBLEMS, SMALL INTESTINE DISORDERS, THYROID, CHILLS, HOT FLASHES, HYPOKINESIA, CHRONIC FATIGUE, EXCESSIVE PERSPIRATION, FACIAL RASH	JOYLESSNESS, UNHAPPINESS, IMPATIENCE	RIGHT NOW, COMMON, QUICKLY, FAST, LATER, "WE'LL SEE"	SLIGHTLY HOT AND RED FOODS, ANTIOXIDANTS, FIRE FOODS, BEING PHYSICALLY ACTIVE, USE OF THE COLOR RED
EARTH	SPLEEN, STOMACH, PANCREAS, SALIVA, MOUTH, MUSCLES	STOMACH-RELATED DIGESTIVE DISORDERS, DIABETES, PANCREATIC DISORDERS, BLOOD CELL PRODUCTION DISORDERS, MUSCULAR DISORDERS	TENSION, EMOTIONAL FLUCTUATIONS	MORE, MOST, "I WISH", MUCH, "IN MY CONTROL," "I'M ON IT" NECESSARY, COMPULSORY, EVERY, ALWAYS, DITTO	GRAINS, CEREALS, PROTEINS, MILDLY SWEET FLAVORS, WARM FOODS, USE OF THE COLOR YELLOW
METAL	LUNGS, LARGE INTESTINE, NOSE, SKIN, RESPIRATORY SYSTEM, EXCRETORY SYSTEM	LARGE INTESTINE DISORDERS, ASTHMA, ALLERGIES, COMMON COLD, SKIN-RELATED PROBLEMS, IMMUNE SYSTEM DISORDERS	SORROW, SADNESS	"I'M AWARE," "I KNOW IT," BUT, HOWEVER, ALTHOUGH, DESPITE, "LET IT STAY," "LET'S KEEP IT," "I CAN'T LET GO OF IT," "I CAN'T GIVE IN," "IT'LL COME IN HANDY"	SPICY AND PUNGENT FOODS, PROBIOTICS, ROOT VEGETABLES, ALKALI FOODS, WHITE-COLORED FOODS SUCH AS ONION, GARLIC, GINGER, MINT, EUCALYPTUS, KALE, CAULIFLOWER, RADISH, LEEK
WATER	KIDNEYS, BLADDER SYSTEM, URINARY TRACT, BLOOD FLUID, OVARIES, PROSTATE, ALL BODILY FLUIDS, EARS, BONES	HORMONAL DISORDERS; DISEASES RELATED TO KIDNEYS AND URINARY TRACT; GENITAL DISORDERS; BONE DISORDERS; HAIR GREYING AND LOSS; BLACKNESS UNDER THE EYES	FEAR, ANXIETY	"I'M AFRAID," "I WORRY THAT…," "IF THAT HAPPENS…," "I AM PANICKING"	SOOTHING HERBAL TEAS, ALL TYPES OF BEANS, GRAINS, NATURAL SALT, WATER, BREATHING EXERCISES, REGULATION OF SLEEP RHYTHM

Daily Cycle

In the natural process of life, we experience the flow we see in the seasons during the day. When the functioning of the body clock follows this flow, you can be healthier.

Having a bowel movement between five and seven in the morning makes the bowels healthier; and having breakfast between seven and eleven in the morning, starting with a light sweet food, activates and strengthens the stomach, pancreas, and spleen.

Staying away from excessive exercise between eleven a.m. and three p.m., and protecting yourself from extreme heat is good for the health of the heart.

Consuming plenty of fluids between three and seven p.m., drinking herbal teas, eating fruits and nuts are good for the health of the kidneys and bladder.

Socializing between seven and eleven p.m. and being in places where you feel happy support the circulatory system and the health of the heart.

It is good for a healthy liver and gallbladder to stay away from meals between eleven p.m. and three a.m., and to be calm and serene. This way, the fat metabolism works at full performance. In this part of the day, stay away from fear, tension, as well as movies, documentaries, or news that makes you anxious.

Make sure to be sound asleep between three and five in the morning. This will allow the body to connect with many cells overlooked during the day that need repairing; it will also allow the mind to calm down and receive the charging energy of life.

Cycle of Life Span

Wood element is the representative of birth,
fire element of childhood,
earth element of adulthood,
metal element of maturity, and
water element of old age and death.

You should remember that when you act in harmony with the life cycle, all systems heal by supporting each other whereas when you resist the cycle, diseases and problems may occur in your body, emotions and thoughts. Both harmony and disharmony are in your hands. Although knowledge is important, being able to use and apply it is much more valuable.

Not being able to leave an item in life and not leaving what needs to be sent out of the body is the result of the same energy frequency. Basically, the action that cannot be executed is to let go. Therefore, you should remember the eventual effects in your body of what you have experienced when you could not let go of a state, and you should focus your awareness on yourself. The first and foremost material possession you have that will keep you comfortable in this life is your body. The more you value it, the more enjoyable it will be for you to savor your experiences.

It is normal for you to be saddened by what you experience when you encounter an unwanted event. You may want to stay in this abnormal sadness, almost as if you want to destroy yourself. At the end of this state, you will have wasted your body's fuel. Health is your most important wealth. You are here as long as you breathe: while that breath is connecting you to life, you should remember that your healthy connection with it also nourishes your body. The first thing you do during events that cause such intense effects as emotional fluctuation or trauma is to hold your breath. Below, I recommend an exercise for you so that you can figure out which area in your body is not nourished and with which energy field you have a weak connection.

Breathing Exercise

Lie on your back on the floor in a quiet place. Take an object weighing about one kilogram (2.2 pounds) and place it first over your heart. Leave it there for thirty seconds, watch it move. Then put the weight below your ribs and watch it move for another thirty seconds. Then put it on your navel and watch the movement for thirty seconds. Finally, try the same thing by placing it below the navel, between the pelvis and the belly button. Determine where the object you use moves less and where it moves more.

If there is little movement in your heart area, you have problems with the heart and the fire element. Your joy of life may have decreased, you may be experiencing emotions about feeling less loved.

If you have little movement under the ribs, you may have problems with decision-making. You should take care of the health of your stomach and pancreas.

▶

If the movement is felt less in the umbilical region, there may be situations where you cannot let go and digest a matter. There may be a disruption in the functioning of the large intestines and the immune system.

If you feel little movement in the underbelly area, when you focus on the things you worry about, you probably feel them right under your nose. Imbalance in sexual energy, low energy may occur.

If all of these points where you have placed the weight work in harmony and balance, like a wave hitting the shore, you are healthy emotionally and physically. If only one or two of them have a good rhythm and the others have a low rhythm, the balance is still broken. An overworked area draws energy from another. Let's assume that only the area between the belly button and the ribs goes up and down, and there is no movement elsewhere. In this case, it is possible to say that there is an excessive desire for control and self-defense. Therefore, stomach ailments and, accordingly, deterioration in the water system and sexual energy balance may occur.

Reading by Examining the Flow of Breath

Talking while holding your breath or feeling short of breath while speaking signifies the emotional pressure that you put on yourself.

Breathing too fast is you feeling restricted in one area, and being late for a matter.

If you mostly breathe through your mouth and have trouble breathing through your nose, it is difficult for you to accept someone else's authority.

If your right nostril is blocked, you cannot accept the developments in financial matters and the flow of life as they are. If the left nostril is blocked or you have trouble breathing, you may not follow your intuition and have a hard time listening to your inner voice.

If only the upper part of the chest moves when you breathe and the breath does not descend to the lower part, it is difficult for you to make decisions on your own, you cannot activate your logic, so your emotions are steering you.

If only your upper abdomen moves when you breathe, you see yourself as the decision center. Being strong and having power are important to you.

PART V

READING LIFE BY EXAMINING THE BODY

What is the Message Physical Features Give?

While reading this book right now, focus on your posture, the form your body has taken. Is it to the left or to the right of the center of gravity; is your neck and back leaning forward; are your shoulders low or backward, are the shoulders raised or tense; are the legs crossed; are any of the toes tense, is there any part of the body that is tense or contracted; how is your face?

These tell about your stance towards life. Now, focus on yourself at different times in your life up to today; what stance do you display while walking, sitting, or working?

Posture and Walk

If your shoulders are low, the weight of your life circumstances is putting you under pressure. If you are squeezing your ribcage by bringing your shoulders forward, you may not be feeling loved. If you have a hump on your back because of your posture, you may be having trouble taking the responsibilities of life.

If you are bringing your chest forward by throwing your shoulders back, you need to show yourself. You are experiencing the fear of not being able to stand out, not being valued, and not being able to show your difference.

If you are walking looking at the ground, you have thoughts and feelings that are pulling you down.

If you raise your head a little too high while walking and your chin is not parallel to the ground but higher up, you do not feel valued enough in a certain area. You are projecting this feeling outward in the form of contempt for others.

If your neck is ahead of your body while walking, you are rushing, blaming yourself for being late and lingering. The incorrect posture of the neck affects the entire spine and this may cause a herniated disc in the future.

The neck tilting to the right while standing or walking shows the person's resistance to material matters, and the tilting to the left shows the resistance to the inner voice.

If a woman is flexible and agile in her walk, she is analytical and productive in life.

If a man takes strong and decided steps while walking, and if his arms and legs are in harmony, it means that he is confident.

Face and Expressions

All parts of the face are associated with an emotion and an organ.

Facial lines and wrinkles, formed by the repetition of the electrical effects of emotions and thoughts, tell us in what condition which of our organs is. It also gives information about our tendencies and what kind of a program we were born with. Color changes on the face are an indication of emotional states.

For example, whitening of your face indicates that you are unable to absorb or digest an event. This affects the lungs and large intestines and indicates that there is a problem with the metal element in the body.

Your face being red is related to the heart and circulatory system. In particular, excessive redness of the sides of the nose and the front of the cheeks, and the formation of fine lines due to the strain of the blood vessels in that area indicate that there is a strain on the heart. You may be pushing yourself because you act in haste and hurry.

If the face is yellow, it tells us about stomach problems. The urge to control is dominant.

A nearly black darkening on the face, especially under the eyes indicates kidney and bladder disorders. There can be a state of fear and a feeling that pulls you down on a subject.

Pimples appearing anywhere on the face indicate a constrained liver and anger in emotion. In the same way, moles on any part of the face are related to the liver and the feeling of anger.

Now go in front of the mirror and examine your face as if you were seeing it for the first time. Find the differences between the right and left sides of your face, identify where your spots, stains, lines, and pimples, if any, are located. Then look at your face again and feel what the dominant emotion is. What is in there? Sadness, joy, sorrow or happiness? Let's evaluate what we have found together.

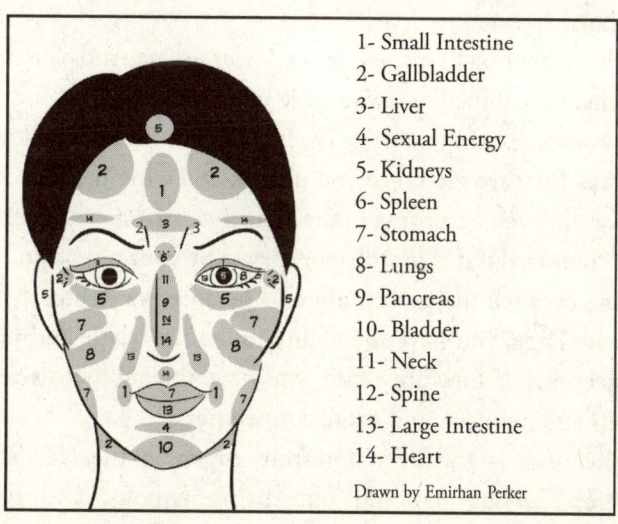

1- Small Intestine
2- Gallbladder
3- Liver
4- Sexual Energy
5- Kidneys
6- Spleen
7- Stomach
8- Lungs
9- Pancreas
10- Bladder
11- Neck
12- Spine
13- Large Intestine
14- Heart

Drawn by Emirhan Perker

The right side of your face represents the masculine side, and the left represents the feminine side. The part under your eyes represents your kidneys and their health status organ wise, and your fears emotion wise. Just below the eye bags and above the cheekbones, your stomach and the power to make decisions are represented. The cheekbones and just below them represent the lungs and the ability to take from life. Your nose represents your heart and joy, and your nasal bone represents your spine and your stance towards life. The small intestine and the heart are represented just below the nose and above the lip. Your upper lip represents your stomach, and your lower lip your intestines. The edges of the lips represent the small intestines. The part under the lip all the way down to your lower jawline represents the bladder and sexual hormones. The gallbladder is represented right under the chin and on the jowl. Your forehead represents not only the liver but also the gallbladder. The root of the nose between the two eyebrows represents the spleen. Now, according to what I have told you, you can read the spots, marks, lines, and moles on your face you have detected.

The formation of a crack in the lower lip may indicate thirst and digestive difficulty in the large intestine.

Moles forewarn that there is a blockage in the energy flow in the area they are on. Once you understand what message they are sending you according to the zone they are on, you can have them removed if it is found appropriate by your physician.

The eyes tell the perception and perspective of life. If your eyes are large, you have the ability to see the whole and make connections; if they are small, you have the ability to see the details and nuances, and make connections.

The nose is the most forefront organ in the face. It is, therefore, about standing out, being famous, and being recognized in your field. It is important that you breathe very easily with the shape of your nose, and that your natural shape is accepted and preserved. It would be beneficial for the person to consider these before having a reduction rhinoplasty. Now look in the mirror again! Divide your face into three parts: the upper part from the eyebrows to the hairline, the middle part between the eyebrows and the bottom of the nose, and the lower part from the bottom of the nose to the tip of the chin. Which part of the face stands out and takes up the larger area:

The upper part; you are using your mind and intellect heavily.

The middle part; you are using your emotions heavily.

The bottom part; you're using your willpower, ambition, or ego heavily.

Balance is always the greatest strength. Strengthening the weaker side makes it easier for you to set the balance.

***

Areas of unwanted hair growth on the face of women indicate blockages in the related meridians and elements. The hair on the chin points to the bladder; under the nose to hormones; and on the cheeks to the lungs. The lack of hair in the beard areas in men indicates hormonal problems.

Hands and Feet

Feet indicate your progress in life, your advancement, and your stability in a subject. There are reflex points of all organs and systems on the soles of the feet, which I share in the image below.

If your big toe is big, you have a strong liver; if your second toe is long, you have a strong stomach; if your smallest toe is long and strong, you have a strong bladder and water system. If you get calluses on the outer edge of your little toe, you are putting pressure on yourself in sexual matters due to learned patterns. Calluses on the feet indicate that there are blockages related to the energy flow of the relevant organ.

Bunions indicate blood contamination and a gossiping habit.

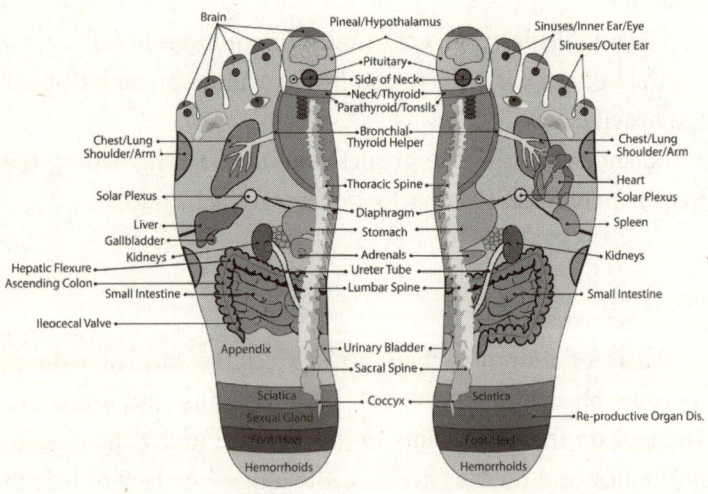

Take one of your old shoes and examine it. Which areas of the sole are more worn out? If the front part is worn, you are in too much of a hurry. You may be using the words "Come on, quickly, faster, more and most..." a lot. If the outer part on the right side of the shoe is worn, it means there is anger against the future and authority. If the left side is worn, you are angry with the past and financial matters. If the heel is worn, there is a fear that blocks the energy of the ovaries, prostate, and kidneys. The wear on the inside of the shoe is related to the bowels, indicating the presence of undigested events and emotions.

Years ago, my neighbor's mother fell ill, and despite long tests and examinations, they kept going to the hospital for weeks with complaints of fatigue and weakness due to anemia. One day, I went to visit them. His mother's face was pale. I could not help but notice the deep crack in her upper lip. The doctors had not yet found the source of the problem, and this made her even more tired. I said it might be the stomach because the signs were telling me she had a sore in her stomach. Her face was yellow, she had a crack in the upper lip and a wound in the middle of the pointer toe. She probably had a large stomach sore, which could be affecting her iron absorption. The patient's daughter and my neighbor, who is a professor at the university, objected to this. They said all the blood tests were done. However, I would realize that they had been listening to me despite their objections when my neighbor knocked on my door a week later. His mother had been diagnosed with a large ulcer in her stomach, and problems larger than anemia were on the verge of starting. Diagnosis made at the right time accelerated the results of the treatment. Curiously, he asked me: "How did you learn about this premonition system?" I explained to him that this was not a premonition system, but a system of reading the signs.

Hands basically symbolize spiritual and physical abilities. Those with long fingers are prone to arts and crafts, and those that are shorter than normal indicate the feeling of being blocked. Accidents and cuts related to the hands are caused by an unconscious desire to punish oneself due to self-blame. Burns indicate burning anger and rage; inflammations indicate fury; warts mean that you do not approve of yourself and find yourself not beautiful enough.

The thumb is related to mind and intelligence. Its positive emotion is trust, and negative emotion is anxiety. The index finger represents the boundaries of ego and personal space. Its positive feeling is, "I know what I want," "I know and protect my space;" Its negative feeling is this thought: "Be as I say and do as I say." It shows the desire to control. The middle finger is about taking action, moving forward. Its positive emotion is tolerance, and the negative one is anger at the inability to do something and what prevents it from being done. The ring finger represents partnership and marital relationship. It represents both the excitement of those coming together and bonding and agreements. Its negative emotion is disharmony and conflict. The little finger represents those who are loved and bonded with love. The positive emotion is the joy created by love, and the negative emotion is unhappiness and hurt.

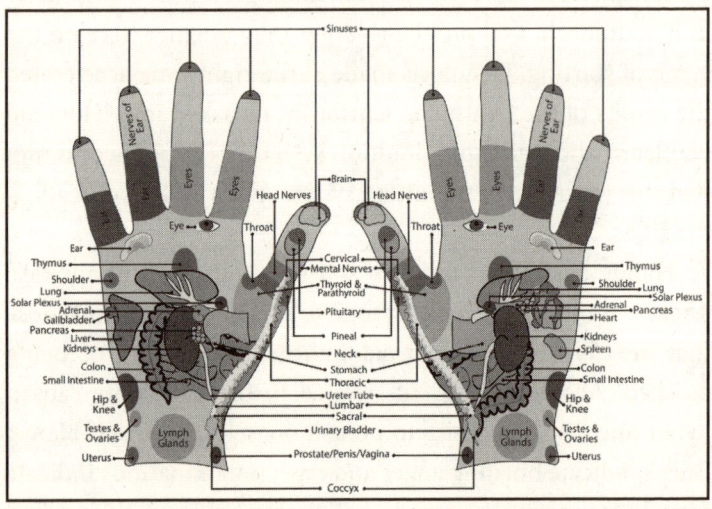

Tongue

The five elements and reflex points, especially the digestive organs, are present in the tongue, too. According to Ayurvedic, the main cause of diseases is the white layer that accumulates on the tongue. This white layer is formed due to excessive acidity and fungus. It is very important to remove this layer by cleaning the tongue every day. Because this whiteness is also a harbinger of poison in the internal organs and digestive disorders. The locations of the bumps, abrasions, splits, scratches, and wounds on the tongue give information about the body's health.

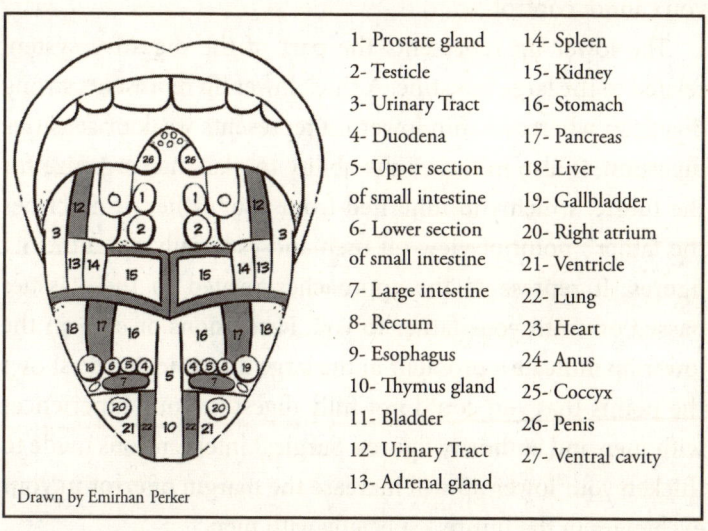

1- Prostate gland	14- Spleen
2- Testicle	15- Kidney
3- Urinary Tract	16- Stomach
4- Duodena	17- Pancreas
5- Upper section of small intestine	18- Liver
6- Lower section of small intestine	19- Gallbladder
7- Large intestine	20- Right atrium
8- Rectum	21- Ventricle
9- Esophagus	22- Lung
10- Thymus gland	23- Heart
11- Bladder	24- Anus
12- Urinary Tract	25- Coccyx
13- Adrenal gland	26- Penis
	27- Ventral cavity

Drawn by Emirhan Perker

Mouth and Teeth

The mouth is the starting point of what we take from life and what we express. Having a big mouth can make you talkative, eager and amenable for life. A thin upper lip indicates a weak stomach, while a thick upper lip indicates a strong stomach.

The upper lip also symbolizes the material side of the father. This represents the impact on you of your father's approach to your mother, as well as the impact of your father's relationships with his mother and with women on you. A scar or mole formed on or around the upper lip represents your troubles in this matter or that your father has aspects that you cannot digest. The operations performed to thicken the lip show that you ignore the messages on the subjects that I have mentioned. Messages that you do not want to see here or even try to get rid of will appear in other areas. These can come into your life in the form of stomach problems, sexual problems, or events that you cannot control.

The lower lip represents the part of the digestive system related to the large intestine. A thick lower lip represents strong digestion whereas a thin lower lip represents weak or sensitive digestion. It also indicates the ability to plan and organize for the future, which you inherited from your father. It describes the father's point of view on men and especially on authority figures. It represents the approaches related to these issues passed on from your father to you. Lacerations or cuts on the lower lip indicate a problem in the large intestine. It also shows the points that you could not fully digest in your experiences with men and authority figures. Surgical interventions made to thicken your lower lip will increase the margin of error in your exchanges in the future, especially with men.

The teeth show your decisions, and the areas in which you are likely to experience stringency or become clearer. Your upper jaw is related to your heritage of paternal behavior and your bond with your paternal relatives. It also reveals your future, your inspirations, and the areas in which you will act. The lower jaw represents the inheritance of behavior from your mother and the bond you have with your maternal relatives.

At the same time, it relates to material issues, traces of past experiences, and your perspective on the world. Mandible and maxillary bites show the balance between masculine and feminine principles.

It is also important which side and teeth you chew with frequently. For example, if you chew more with the left side, it means that your mother, women, matters related to the past, material and money matters, and the situations related to the feminine organs in the body are more important for you. If you are chewing with the right side, you have a more intense agenda about masculine organs in the body, as well as future issues, future expectations, people in authority, men, and your father.

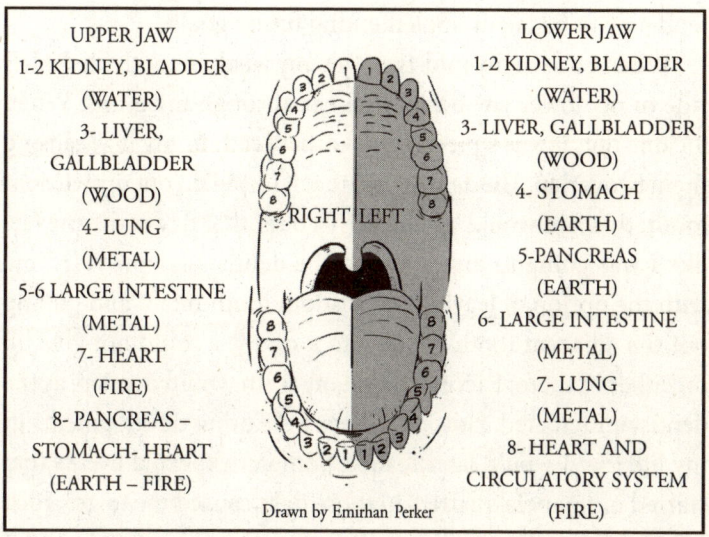

UPPER JAW	LOWER JAW
1-2 KIDNEY, BLADDER (WATER)	1-2 KIDNEY, BLADDER (WATER)
3- LIVER, GALLBLADDER (WOOD)	3- LIVER, GALLBLADDER (WOOD)
4- LUNG (METAL)	4- STOMACH (EARTH)
5-6 LARGE INTESTINE (METAL)	5-PANCREAS (EARTH)
7- HEART (FIRE)	6- LARGE INTESTINE (METAL)
8- PANCREAS – STOMACH- HEART (EARTH – FIRE)	7- LUNG (METAL)
	8- HEART AND CIRCULATORY SYSTEM (FIRE)

RIGHT LEFT

Drawn by Emirhan Perker

The overlapping of the teeth by clenching the lower jaw represents the tightness in financial matters or the intense daily flow, as well as the dependency of the relationship with the mother, a sister or a woman. The gap of the teeth in the lower jaw indicates comfort in financial matters. If they are very distant, this indicates being distant with women and the mother. This also causes a tendency to be slow when assuming responsibility and taking action in life.

The overlapping of the teeth by clenching the upper jaw represents your inability to make the desired progress in the issues related to the future, your tendency to prioritize others, and the past agenda being more important. It also indicates the oppressive effect of the relationships established with the father, men or brothers. The gap between the teeth in the upper jaw means that the chances and opportunities are high in the development of events. If they are too spaced, it means the lack of connection with masculine energy. It is also about the tendency to be lax in implementing future goals.

When I was in my mid-twenties, my wisdom tooth on the left side of my lower jaw began to break through my gums. When it came out, it was squeezing the other teeth in my jaw, causing them to overlap. The dentist said that if he pulled out my wisdom tooth, this jam would be fixed. This offer that day made me feel like I was going to lose a tooth. The dentist also provided me with the option of leaving my wisdom tooth intact and pulling out the adjacent tooth which had a cavity. I could not give up on either of them. I accepted that my teeth would overlap, as the dentist anticipated. However, there were other developments in my life that I would later realize. Some unexpected events that started in financial matters in those days caused me to get stuck many times over the years. This situation continued until I realized that the offer made that day would create a relief in my mouth. I had a somewhat awakening. I went to the dentist and had the molar next to my wisdom tooth extracted. Then I took orthodontic treatment to relieve this overlapping in my lower jaw. The blockade that I applied to myself years ago in financial matters was then lifted.

The most important gain of this experience was my realization that I was putting pressure on myself regarding financial matters.

Another area where self-pressure is revealed is the clenching and grinding of teeth during sleep. It has been seen that people who clench their teeth generally sing the other's tune and stay on their good side, and suppress what they want to do. Teeth grinding, on the other hand, is the projection to the subconscious of the disagreement and conflict between the parents. The person feels stuck and helpless between the two sides. In both cases, one of the parents may have an oppressive or controlling nature. The first step to be taken in order to be able to change this situation is to decide to be free from the pressure that the person unwittingly exerts on himself/herself.

Teeth are about decisions. The pains you suffer related to teeth are caused by your self-blame for not being able to make a decision; and the pus that occurs in the teeth is caused by the anger you experience.

The Meaning of Weights

According to the part where the weight accumulates, the body points out a problem in that part. Any strain, illness or fear from childhood prompts the body to lubricate so that it can protect itself. As long as the need for protection continues, so does the need for lubrication. The adipose tissue, produced as a shield to defend and protect oneself, can easily turn into a healthy state as long as the person can trust himself/herself and life.

1. Fat accumulated in the upper part of the navel is related to anger at the father and men, as well as the lack of a future plan.

2. The fat accumulated in the lower part of the navel is related to the anger felt towards the mother, life, and the body.

3. Abdominal bloating is a sign of undigested emotions, as well as knowledge that has not been put into action.

4. Lubrication on the back is related to the fears that certain difficulties experienced in the past will recur.

5. Fat accumulated in the hip area points to a trust issue due to the bond with the father. Inability to fully relax with the feeling of trust...

6. Fat under the legs indicates a lack of confidence in life, and the feeling of vulnerability due to the bond with an oppressive or overly principled mother.

7. Fat in the upper arms represents an inability to feel loved, ergo vulnerability.

The Choice of Food

Nutrition is about being able to receive and accept
life's offers, beauties, and flavors.
Our diet shows
the form of our behavior in life.

What lies behind the excessive consumption of bakery products is the effect of absence codes. It stems from your concern that the resources at hand will not be enough.

The desire to eat fried foods excessively is the result of the anger for not being able to take action in an area that you demand.

The indulgence in sweet and sugary foods results from the inability to taste the flavors in many areas of life. There is a demand for the repetition of past memories and experiences. There may also be a lack of pleasures that cannot be taken in the emotional or sexual life. When a balanced saturation is reached, the desire to eat excessive amounts of sweets will turn back to normal.

What lies behind the desire to often consume fast food or snacks is a lack of self-worth, self-restraint in some areas, and laziness.

Eating by chewing the food little refers to problems with taking in and digesting events. It means that the person does not dwell on important issues and that they are explored insufficiently.

Those who overeat are fearful and anxious that life does not or may not be able to feed them.

Lack of appetite suggests that there is a lack of passion for life, and an inability to take root; and that opportunities presented are ignored and life is judged.

Not drinking water means not receiving and not being able to accept things.

Finally, excessive alcohol consumption is an indicator of the desire to numb oneself.

PART VI

READING THE POSITIVE AND NEGATIVE

It is Life That Restores the Balance When You Go To Extremes

Let's face it, these days everyone is trying to stay positive all the time. The pressure of "Don't be negative, stay positive!" appears in every platform from books to social media, from television series to programs.

It seems as if positivity is gradually becoming a necessity… "Yes" to everything; "smiley" emoji to everything; "approval" of everything.

In the same token, the pressure that 'it is not good to be negative,' 'that it is shameful to say no' crowns it all…

You have to give whatever anyone wants from you because it is a shame to say "no."

This is how most of us were raised, how we were all taught. What is interesting here is that in Turkish the word "no" did not exist, only the word "alright" did. "No" entered our language later. In the culture we live in, there is a significant problem of not being able to say "no" because it is a social code.

The "yes" and "no" responses of children when asked for something were examined in many parts of the world. It is observed that the gesture that means "no" is shaking the head to the right and left in almost all of them, while the gesture that means "yes" is nodding the head up and down. However, in our culture, the gesture of the expression "yes" is simply to lower the head downwards, while the reaction of the expression "no" is to only raise the head upwards. The conclusion we can draw from this is that our society's approach to saying yes and no is unique.

I was one of those people who just bowed their head, saying "yes." When I was asked for help, I considered it my duty to fulfill it. The knowledge and codes I had received were causing me to behave this way. That is why, until the age of twenty-eight, I consciously stayed away from businesses such as trade where I had to take the initiative. I only worked in consulting and training jobs. I did not know the outside world well enough to trade. In college, my friends used to call me "the happy kid" because I was always positive and would do whatever people around me asked in order to make them happy. However, there is a very important point here. I considered getting help or support from others as a deficiency while describing not being able to give as a negative thing. On the other hand, I thought I knew very well how to give. I thought I was being a positive person by sharing everything that was mine with others, sometimes even giving all that I had. In my opinion, it was not a pleasant thing to receive what was offered whereas to give was one of the most beautiful pleasures of life.

When I was young, I was the health consultant to one of Turkey's leading industrialists. He asked me from time to time, "What can I do for you, what do you need?" When he asked, I was almost numbed and I was having a hard time even answering. I felt helpless in the face of this offer he used to make. In fact, while there were many things I could possibly ask him for my advancement, I kept silent and refused his offer every time. At the time, I was doing my master's degree at Marmara University, Faculty of Health Sciences. The person I mentioned introduced me to the rector of the university, praising me. I was embarrassed by this gesture and his compliments, and I did not feel good at all. In the following years, I better understood why I was uncomfortable with having been praised, and supported by a more powerful and prominent figure than myself, which I could not understand in those days. It was necessary to receive praise, to accept patronage, to "receive" in order to make room for someone else's power. Starting from my thirties, life forcefully taught me how to do the act of "receiving".

Now think about it: when you are offered help in a situation where you have difficulty, do you answer according to the person who makes the offer or according to your own circumstance?

Now let's explore my assumption that giving is superior. I already told you how I had given many things and I was very happy about it. You may think that I was giving the right thing at the right time when I was going to extremes but it was not the situation. As it turns out, on the one hand, there were some things that I did not let go of by gripping them very tightly; and on the other hand, I was squandering my stuff away. I was even hoarding in some areas. Especially books, I could not let go of them although I did not notice it; and I could not even share the ones I thought I would not get in my hands again. The side of me that went to extremes hid things from me. In fact, behind my act of collecting books lied the ideas and decisions that I brought from the past and could not let go of, as well as the knowledge that I laid claims to. The things I had accumulated in terms of this stuff, knowledge, and state had caused a stone formation in my gallbladder and kidneys. Although I started to realize the causes of this issue, coming up with a solution did not happen overnight, since leaving knowledge voluntarily that one has learned and held was not possible by only saying "I am leaving you." This bond had continued until I found out why I needed that attachment. As you can guess, the state of not being able to quit last visited my bowels. The scars of my past experiences that I could not let go of almost made me suffer from high blood pressure.

My university education, sports background, research interest, what I learned from spiritual studies, and the knowledge and experience I gained while helping my consultees were not enough to solve my own problems up to that point because I was focusing only on the outside, separating myself from the outside. Those who were to blame and those responsible were also outside. As soon as I realized that what I saw in the mirror of life told me about myself, I started to look inward at myself. My objections began to decrease and my acceptance began to increase. In fact, I understood that my resistance to receiving was due to my inability to accept what was. As I went to extremes and saw only what I had given, ignoring what I had kept, my favorites were being taken away from me. With my understanding back then, I still could not understand the reason for the negative behaviors I was watching as I did benevolent acts and approached people with positive emotions. Those who sow beauty and goodness should reap the fruits of these. I could not find where I was wrong yet. If those I watched in the mirror were telling me about myself, then was it also me I watched and could not accept? I was very confused; I was denying that they could be my reflections, and was trying to change them and control them so that they could be like me. Of course, things were getting out of control and I was going back to square one. Knowing what to do did not give me the power to implement it. As soon as I stopped saying good or bad, and judging, my perspective changed, my feeling changed, the course of events changed. I understood that the events and people I tried to control were there because I did not trust life and the one who created it. The water was flowing its own stream in the most natural way, and I was the one struggling in vain to swim upstream. This realization calmed me and facilitated my transition to peace and acceptance.

It is life that restores the balance when you go to extremes.

How Would You Know You Have Gone to Extreme Positive?

The biggest positive area is excessive movement, not being able to calm down, controlling events and people, overthinking, and believing that the solution is only in you, and saying "I will handle it."

One day, the son of a relative of mine came to Istanbul from our hometown. He had sold his products and received a check in return. He was negotiating with banks and factoring companies to turn it into cash. I said to him, "Don't pay interest in vain, I'll give you the amount on the check or the money you need. When you collect the check, you will send me the money." So, I gave him the money, and I left the check with him. Although a long time passed, there was no sound from the other side. Therefore, I called him several times on the phone, but to no avail. Then, because of this money exchange, resentment emerged between his family and mine. When I went to my hometown, they felt compelled to run away from me. I learned my lesson: even though there was no demand for help from me, I tried to help someone and hindered his effort.

The basic principle here is to first listen carefully to what is being demanded from you. When you decide to do that help sincerely with the knowledge that you cannot save him with your help, you become the hand that fulfills the demand, and not the hand that gives it, thus the balance is maintained. The help you will provide while seeing the person that demands it as incapable can render you incapable in a certain situation.

How Would You Know You Have Gone to Extreme Negative?

The biggest negative area is where you stay still when you should be moving. If you are resisting innovation and objecting to change in any state and situation, you are in negative energy. It is a habit you have to let go of, a relationship that needs to end but you feel compelled to continue, and things you have been lazy about.

Years ago, we did some work with a consultee whose health deteriorated because he had been spending too much time and energy on his job. At first, he arranged his diet, removed unhealthy and acidic foods from his life, quit smoking, started sports, and detoxified. He also reorganized his daily workflow so he regained his health in a time period as short as a year.

This consultee, who had dedicated himself to his work and resisted change and innovation by remaining inactive in life, gained a brand-new perspective. He took care of himself, played sports and ate healthy. He also started to ignore the problems in the workplace and to stay away from the workplace instead of creating solutions. He carried the irresponsible state he used to treat his body to his workplace. "My financial situation is good; what I have in hand is enough for me. I will sell my business and live a quiet life," he would say. However, he would neither give up on his business nor his comfort. In short, he did not want to move from one stagnant state to another. Life heard him, and the problems at work grew and became visible. Since he could not establish the right rhythm between his work and personal life, and since he could not take on responsibilities, his work life came to the forefront again. The pace of work upon his return made his health deteriorate. Then he called me again. We had had a break from our work for a while. He said he wanted a private session again. My question to him was: "What did you neglect in the meantime, and where did you go to extremes?"

"It turns out that I haven't abandoned my sentiment of 'let it stay the same, let it not change,'" he said. "I just swapped places between my work and my body. My body was cured of cancer but now my job is cancer. Isn't there a balance to it, do I necessarily have to pay a price, when will life be fair to me? If I have a chance, I want to use it. Knowing that I'm back to the old me felt even harder than opening the door to the new."

In response, "Are you in for a fasting of 'let it be,' 'let it stay,' and 'ditto'?" I asked.

As he had kept saying, "Let it be the same," cancer had moved but not gone. In the past, it was in his body, now it was sucking its energy from his work and relationships. "If you are ready to let go of sameness, life will light your way again," I said.

He made the necessary arrangements in his work; he always focused on the result even though he felt pain while leaving certain things; he initiated the movement on the issues he stopped; and so his life got into balance, sending the cancer frequency away from his life.

When you go to extremes in action or inaction, you can attract problems or illnesses into your life in order to restore your balance. When you want to avoid them, ignore them, fear confrontation, and do not receive their message, as I explained in the previous anecdote, cancer can move from one place to another. Sometimes it can pass from your body to your job or relationships, sometimes to your income, and sometimes even to your moral world. Since problems cannot convey their message every time you wave them off, they increase their effects in a such way to attract your attention. This can cause a result similar to the sudden bursting of a balloon that has been inflated to its breaking point.

We call such messages "accidents." Whether it is an event accident, a bodily accident or a traffic accident... It does not matter... Whatever you have been doing, thinking, or trying to do at the moment the accident happened, you would stop and give your full attention to the moment of the accident. Now all your focus is on the point where the accident affects you. Whether you have hurt your hand, or fallen off the bike, or received the news of a loss, all other issues would lose their importance at that moment and the accident would come to the forefront. Maybe you were working in the morning without even having breakfast because of your busy schedule that day, but now the impact of the accident puts aside the work that even kept you from eating. In fact, this life is reaching out to you, making you look at yourself from the mirror of the accident.

"Look at this mirror, you are here as long as you see yourself in this mirror. Remember yourself!
One day, you may not even find this body to remind you of yourself.
Take your hands off the one who pulls you away from you. Look at yourself!
If you are here, all will be solved; remember to ask for help, let us support you, everything is fine if you are in it!"

An accident is a discharge of energy. Its power and effect last as long as it has been accumulating. Sometimes it happens to societies, sometimes to communities, sometimes only to the individual.

An accident is a positive energy as it expresses a sudden action. However, it establishes the balance by flowing to the one who has only been giving or receiving for a long time, namely to the one who has been objecting.

I was a successful athlete in national and international competitions until the age of nineteen. I used to see competition and rivalry as a factor that strengthens the ego and increases ambition. Then I decided to quit competing. But despite my decision, for months I kept running from one competition to another wherever there was one. This side of me, which was going against my own decision, caused me various accidents and injuries. Each of my resistances was creating a new injury. As a result of the rupture of my shoulder ligaments, my shoulder was dislocated many times during competitions. It was as if these injuries were saying to me, "Get out of this area." When my arm bone could no longer sit in the shoulder sling, the incident and the body accident made me enforce my decision: "The competition period was over."

My right shoulder was dislocated, preventing me from going down the wrong path, as I was drifting away from my life's purpose and steering out of the way I was supposed to go. Thanks to this incident, I remembered my life's purpose at an early age and started my coaching practice. It made me feel good to guide those who needed support and knowledge on a subject that I was well-versed in, and demanded help from me. The methods I was seeking in order to heal my torn muscles, about which I was so stubborn that I almost had to have surgery, lead me to knowledge that could be useful to other people.

Accidents come so as to neutralize energy. Earthquakes and natural disasters also remove and cleanse the accumulated negative energy. You must have witnessed how calm people are after natural disasters.

When you have drifted away from your own center and your own purpose and path, all kinds of sudden exertions and influences from outside serve you in order for you to return to your own center.

Extremes are not just about giving and receiving. Lingering too long, not wanting to get out of the mood you are in is also excessiveness. You go to extremes when you cling to the influence of an event that you experienced in the past, when you live and breathe with it, and even when you want to build your future with that influence. Every repetition turns into a routine, and routines turn into addictions. Actions, thought patterns, and expressions that you repeat over and over create stagnation and keep you inactive. All kinds of procrastination and laziness keep you from moving forward into the future. This is the result of your willingness to stop or even reverse life as it is constantly moving forward. There could be experiences you have left behind but want to relive again, which make you feel good, safe, and beautiful. Or on the contrary, there may be events that you do not like when they are mentioned and you fear that they will repeat. Whether you want or fear that they repeat and avoid stepping into the new, the "ditto" frequency governs you. It governs not only you, but also your relationships, your home, your job, your expressions, your choices, that is whatever reflects from you. Repeating the past is the easy option for your mind. Anchoring in the past by choosing the easy and the familiar is to be imprisoned in the past. At the root of your desire to stay in the past are the issues that you cannot understand and resolve about the matter, body, and mother. It is that you want life and your mother to feed you without you having to move or take action. You want to connect with the past by sensing the flavors of your childhood and remembering your experiences, so you are making moves to recreate the environments in the past or you are constantly complaining about the past.

The drive of the past continues until you are able to stand on your own two feet, meet your needs and make your choices of your own free will. If your past fears are recurring or you cannot let go of the fear, you may experience kidney, bladder problems, as well as sexual disorders. Events in life unfold the way you fear them to. Constantly talking about a sadness you have experienced in the past creates discomfort in your respiratory system and lungs.

Expressions such as "let it stay, let it be, we will need it, we will do it later..." strengthen the state of being in the past and not being able to let go. Life reaches out to activate and balance you from this stillness and invites you to your center. The stronger the bond and the greater the resistance, the harsher you will feel the help that has come. This help can support you to let go of that state, sometimes in the form of an illness, sometimes problems in a relationship, sometimes a loss, or a financial problem.

If you have mental or physical activity that goes to extremes, especially if you get too caught up in the hustle and bustle of life, if you do not leave any spare time for yourself and give your priority to the outside or to others, it means you have started living for the future. Today and tomorrow are full of schedules, tasks and you still have things to do, but time is not enough for you. You have begun to borrow days from the future. In such cases, your capacity to take root in life and in the moment you are living weakens. Since you cannot keep up with the assignments you have started, you become unable to complete them. A lot of unfinished business and work piles up. Yet, you start new assignments again. Living in the future is about not being able to feed on the roots of the past, and about father issues. The central point here is your father. Whether you are very fond of your father, or away from your father, or complaining about him, the main subject is the father. The fear of rebelling against him or going against the rules he has set determines the severity of the problem in this area.

When living your life by postponing it to the future by moving away from the present, you attempt to speed things up with the feeling of being late. You often use phrases like "Right now, quick, come on, I don't have time, I have a lot of work to do." The reason for this is that you want to slow yourself down.

Living in the future is not to be in the present. Now, that is the time you are in, is the center of you and your life. When you increase your speed, thinking that you will go faster than the rhythm of life, you invite the actions that will stop this tempo, bring you to the center, and that will make you give priority to yourself.

In these cases, mostly cardiovascular problems, high blood pressure, and fatigue-related disorders are experienced. Sometimes a balance is restored with a crash that occurs in one area. It can be an economic, physical, or emotional crash.

Whether you are a materialist or a spiritualist, whether you are closer to your mother or father, whether you live in the past or in the future, they are all signs that you are far from your center.

As you notice that areas that seem to be very different in life
actually have similar characteristics,
your admiration for the magnificent mathematics
of the universe will increase.

The effort to know oneself and understand life has been the most important issue since ancient times.

So, how does a person know himself?

Obviously, it is possible to know yourself from your physical body, health, experiences, choices, emotions, relationships, and external projections.

Your mother, father, and the family you have grown up in is the area where you were first shaped. You define yourself with them. You bear the surname of your parents and position yourself as part of society with this identity information. Your first memories, traumas, joys, dreams, and future goals were shaped by family. When you assess yourself within the bond you have with your family, you will find the answers to many of your identity questions.

What Reflects from Your Family

Your rank among your siblings, the professional or social status of your parents, the environment you have been raised in, the geographical location, and changes you have been through have all had an impact on the choices you have made throughout your life, whether you are aware of it or not. You may have got used to financial difficulties, and you may not even be able to escape from them even if you want to; you may be cheated on in your relationships, you may be abandoned or you may be attracting people who treat you badly. When you see the source of these, you also get the key to transforming them. You can free yourself from the behavior patterns you have got used to and been repeating by learning from your family.

A good diagnosis paves the way to recovery.

The authority figure you have watched in your family determines who you will take seriously as an authority figure in the future. If the father is the one who sets the rules and dominates at home, the state and the divine system will be the authority for you. You will accept a man as the authority. If it is the mother who sets the rules and dominates at home, the authoritative power in life will be material laws and economic issues. You will accept a woman as an authority. If you are the one who does not recognize and stands against the rules in the family, you will have problems with the principles represented by the authority figure of whomever you see as an authority in the following years.

If there are parental conflicts in the family model you are watching, chronic respiratory system ailments, teeth grinding, posture and spine disorders may occur. You will need personal relations in which you will repeat the model you have watched and learned. In your social circle, you will be among the people with whom you will be in conflict.

If there has been someone in the family model who has had an oppressive attitude towards you, you will need that pressure in the coming years. If that family member is a man, you will feel pressure from men; if it is a woman, you will feel pressure from women.

If a girl has been pressured by her father or a man in the family, she needs a rule-making mechanism or a man who oppresses or compels her to do what he wants. This pressure can sometimes make that girl excessively strict, or it can have the opposite effect, making her someone who does not recognize rules and has problems with laws and rules. Large intestine and gall bladder problems may occur in the body.

If a girl has been pressured by her mother or a woman in the family, she will need pressure in financial matters, business life, as well as physical and emotional matters. She will be under pressure from and have problems with her supervisor at work, from her teacher at school, and from her mother-in-law in marriage. Since this pressure, which she has learned and got used to, will also suppress her self-expression, so she may experience problems in the thyroid and throat area, or diseases in the uterus and ovaries. She will apply this oppressive attitude towards herself and want to control the flow of life; consequently, she may experience various disorders in organs such as the stomach and pancreas.

If a boy has been pressured by the father or a man in the family, he will need outside pressure to move forward into the future. This pressure can often come from government agencies and laws, political or religious authorities. It causes conflicts and power struggles for the person with the rule-making men. In personal relationships, he will display an oppressive attitude, trying to get what he asks done. He needs people around him who criticize and put pressure on him. This can cause gallbladder and large intestine problems in the body.

If the boy has been pressured by the mother or a woman in the family, he will have worries about financial matters. He will need people or events in his business life that will put pressure on him. Because of his need for female authority, he will choose a spouse or partner who will make him feel pressured financially or sexually. He will invest by taking out loans. His body will experience stomach and pancreatic disorders, sexual problems, as well as fattening in the lower abdomen and kidney area.

If someone is abused in the family, the fact that the abuse was from their own or the opposite sex will affect the defense mechanisms they will develop to protect themselves. When a child is physically or sexually abused by a woman in the family, this creates repetitive abuse energy in different areas.

They may experience bankruptcy in financial matters, loss through theft, inability to claim their rights, severe diseases in the body or loss of limbs. Anger may occur towards their own sex or the opposite sex.

A girl who is physically or sexually abused by the opposite sex will experience intense worries about her future; she can struggle with authorities such as the state, school, and workplace; and she may struggle with problems that will eventually cause her loss. Anger against her own or the opposite sex may occur.

Another situation in which a person feels worthless, pressured and unprotected is when the mother becomes pregnant again while breastfeeding. The mother directs some of the resources in her body to her unborn child. Having to share their mother after birth can make children feel abused. As a result, rivalry and strife can occur between siblings. This causes those people to compete with others of the same gender as their siblings at a later age. Let's say you are a sister and your sibling is also a girl. For your little sister, you are someone who should share your resources with her. For you, there is an obligation to give what you have to your sister. However, neither of you are satisfied with this situation, but you have difficulty changing your behavioral preferences. The sentence you often hear in the family is, "Share what you have with your sister!"

This principle works in reverse when the age gap between siblings widens. The younger sister gives what she has to the older sister to get her approval, and the older sister will take it. Here the younger one assumes the role of the older sister.

***

One day, one of my consultees said that she constantly had conflicts with women at work and wanted to solve the problem. When she was only one year old, her mother became pregnant with her sister. With the birth of her sister, her mother gave all her attention to the younger sister, and my consultee felt quite alone. During our session, she remembered that she had some problems with her sister to get her mother's attention. She realized that she had problems with female employees in order to attract the attention of her supervisor at work because of the attention-grabbing pattern she had learned, and thus she solved her problem.

Another consultee said that her marriage was not going well and that she was constantly fighting with her husband. She was asking for support to end the marriage. She told me that her husband was not interested in her. She admitted that she did not feel like a woman. Her husband was a loyal, hardworking and honest man. The woman had servants at home and did not have to do housework. All she wanted was for her hardworking husband to show interest in her when he came home, compliment her and be active in the community life along with her. I asked her to tell me what a normal day at home was like. When she said, "Our father gets up very early," I said, "There is no need to continue, the problem is clear." She had put her husband in her father's place. Then I asked her to tell me about her relationship with her father. She noted: "My father comes from a very kind, gentle, and noble family indeed. He is very fond of me, he pampers me, we have a lot of fun together. He is a well-respected man with a wide social circle." As for her relationship with her mother, she explained: "My mother was a very well-groomed, young-looking, social woman. She was a little selfish and a little grumpy; she and my father could not get along very well."

When I asked her which parent she felt close to, she said, "My father, of course. He is both my friend and my greatest assurance."

This experience of my consultee, in fact, included the principles that guide most people's relationships. My consultee actually took her mother as a role model, but the male model was her father. Since she could not put any other man in her father's place in her life, she referred to her husband as "father".

At one point in our conversation, she remembered that her mother, whom she did not feel close to and disapproved of, also addressed her husband as "father." That was the moment of real awakening. She started sobbing. She confessed that she was about to end her marriage because she tried to make it resemble the environment of the family she was born into. She stopped and suddenly began to count her traits that resembled her mother. She changed her mind about getting divorced after our sessions.

One day, a father came to complain that his son was using alcohol and drugs. He wanted to save his son. He told me that he had desperately tried everything he could, but to no avail. I told him that I could help him if he wanted, and not his son. He insisted that his son needed help and that he did not have any demands for himself. And I said to him, "Those who are not thirsty are not given water by force, and those who do not demand help are not helped." He left, with some reproach. He came back a month later and said why he was experiencing such a predicament and wanted to be rid of it. He had begun to see himself in the mirror now.

I asked him to describe his relationship with his own father. "My father was a well-liked and respected industrialist, and he would come home very late because he worked very hard. He didn't spend much time with me and my mother. When he spent time at home, he would pass out on the sofa from exhaustion. All he knew was work" he said.

"Well, what do you do?" I asked.

"My job is to collect the rental income from the family. This income is more than sufficient, there is no need for another job" he replied.

When I asked him, "What does your son do?" his answer was, "He was a smart and hardworking boy, he followed the friends he met in business life, and although there is no one in the family who is fond of alcohol, my son uses both alcohol and drugs, and he has lost his job, too. I take care of him, and he makes me pay for the poisons he uses."

"Is your son like his grandfather?"

"No, not at all. My father was very disciplined. He did nothing but work. My naughty son does nothing but drink."

"So, we can say there's an area where they both can do nothing but numb themselves with something?"

He did not answer.

He identified his son with his father. When I said this, he objected.

"Work for your father, alcohol for your son, comfort for you," I said. "These are the areas where you forget and lose yourselves. Places where you numb yourselves. This is called numbness..."

He suddenly jumped up from his seat and left grumbling. A month or two passed, my assistant passed me a note that he wanted an appointment. When we met again, a completely different man was sitting before me. He was softened, serene, and ready to listen.

He actually wanted to raise his son with more freedom because his father had suppressed him. Because his father worked so hard, my consultee never wanted to work. I pointed out that when he stopped judging his father and son, the problem between them would be resolved. When he stopped being angry with his father, he realized that he was like his father. In fact, it was himself with whom he was fighting in the mirror. The moment he finished his battle with himself, he disciplined his son and stopped being his drug sponsor; and things got back on track.

Who is your family role model, who have you been influenced by, how close are you to the role model you object to? When you ask these questions to yourself and sincerely seek answers, you will find solutions that will shed light on your path. This way, you will have found the treasures of the family whose roots you come from, as well as what is in the legacy that has been passed on to you. The reason for this is that with the choices you make, you copy what you see and experience by drawing from the models that you sometimes avoid, sometimes try to imitate. However, none of these models are you. Of course, you have grown up with what you have seen from your family, but you have the right to make your own future plans. The easy thing to do is to keep the old one going. Although this will challenge you at first, the state in which you will be happy and evolve is your originality. Your authenticity will light your way.

***

One of my followers, who sent me an e-mail, had been watching my YouTube videos, trying to apply some of the knowledge I shared, but could not achieve the exact result she desired.

"I understand what you are saying. Yes, I chose my oppressive and conservative mother and father. Now, I want to say that I don't need them anymore. But it's not working. I have to live with them. Why might I have chosen the mother who yells at me every day?"

I added this story below the answer I gave her: A man thought he was a grain of corn. He was very afraid that the chickens would eat him, and wherever he saw a chicken, he would run away. In the end, they confined him to a psychiatric hospital. For a long while, doctors had been trying to convince him that he was not a grain of corn, but actually a human being. During one session, his doctor asked him again.

"Tell me, what are you?"

"I am a human being," answered the man.

"But you used to claim that you were a grain of corn!"

"That was then. Now I know, I'm human."

After this session, his doctors decided to discharge him. With the joy of healing his patient, the man's doctor wanted to give him a ride home. Just as the man was about to enter the house, he saw chickens running around, so he ran away and climbed a tree. The doctor was surprised, of course.

"What are you doing? Why did you climb that tree?" asked the doctor.

"Didn't you see, the chickens were attacking me. I was protecting myself."

"But haven't you learned that you are human? You just told me that you are not a grain of corn anymore, that you are human?"

"Okay, I know I'm not a grain of corn, but do the chickens know that?" replied the man.

Having knowledge is not the same as putting it into practice. With what they learn from books or courses, most people try to change their surroundings, that is the mirror they look in. However, this is a completely futile effort. All knowledge we learn is for us first. We can only speak of its taste on us and share it with those who ask to be at our table. No one else would change with what we learn, but we would see our own rigidity in their resistance.

What Do Your Choices Tell You?

For a while, I could not understand why my father, who had wrestled for a few years in his youth, took me by the hand and introduced me to the sport of Judo when I was nine years old. A year after I started judo, I began to comprehend why this sport was important to me.

I worked out with masters on the 8th dan, which is 8 ranks higher than the black belt. They taught me techniques and exercises that even many of my trainers did not know at that time. I had other role models apart from the behavioral patterns I learned from my family. My masters were strict, they set rules and taught me to stay centered. There was no trace of my pampered self as the only child and almost the only grandchild in the family. As we approached mastery, we simplified the effort and strengthened the balance.

I also started other Far Eastern sports at that time, but I did not have a grasp of the philosophy of any of them at that time. I was just applying with great pleasure and pride what I had learned at the level of movement. But years later, I learned and comprehended that behind these movements there are self-knowledge and the balance laws of life.

In fact, what I needed to learn was balance. While I was telling others to stay in balance, to be balanced, I was learning, too. The choice of sport I made showed my lack of balance between spirit and matter. More importantly, when he held my hand, took me to that gym, and had me start sports, I felt that my father, who I thought was not interested in me, was actually only interested in me. The medals I received in all the competitions I participated in and later the diplomas that I earned served to strengthen the bond I had established with him, and they were all displayed as a wall of pride in his restaurant. It was only much later that I realized why for years I had a hard time quitting judo. I did not want to let go of the hand of my father, whom I thought was not interested in me on the outside and even blamed me. Because he was fathering everyone else, he could not see his own son. Maybe that is why medals and diplomas were right in front of him. He might also have thought that he was showing me interest and doing me a favor by keeping his distance from me. Because I blamed my father, my daughter, who was five months old in her mother's womb when my father died, became a mirror for me in the following years.

Now let's go back and look at your interests... What kind of services do your education, sports, hobbies, entertainment, taste of music and your other choices that you think you have picked by chance, or maybe even forced or unintentionally chosen provide you with? These laws also apply to your choice of friends. The Turkish proverb "Tell me who your friend is and I will tell you who you are..." is also a reminder that directs people to read from their choices.

Who Do You Become Complete With?

You must have wondered why your mom and dad chose each other. There were some reasons that brought them together even if they were in conflict, separated, resentful, or did not see each other for years. Of course, this unification, whether arranged or voluntary, has had good days and bad days. Maybe you took the side of one of them, and maybe you still do.

Just as the days get longer, the nights get shorter, and the days get shorter when the nights get longer in the seasonal cycles, the same system works in the masculine and feminine principles of life. It is like the completion of a day. The one who speaks a lot meets the one who speaks little, the one who is meticulous meets the one who is messy, the dominant one meets the one who is passive. For example, conflict arises when two loudmouths come together and if one party does not keep quiet to listen to the other party. When two dominants come together and want to have a say in the same matter, again conflict arises. If those who come together by being completed with one another for a purpose, for destiny's plan, their togetherness does not turn into a match unless they harmonize. When these parties continue to stay together, they begin to conflict from the inside and to be completed from the outside. For instance, if the woman feels her femininity is lacking, she takes her mother-in-law or her own mother into the house or pushes the man to other women. The relationship is completed with external support, the coupling continues with the help of a cane.

A consultee of mine got married after dating his wife for a long time. They got along well, and two months after their marriage, his wife became pregnant. My client, who was a manager, became unemployed when his wife was four months pregnant. Within a few months, they had to move to another city. He started working and his wife had to stay at home to take care of the child. They did not want to entrust the child to anyone in a town where they did not have a social circle. The tension created by so many changes developed in a short time and was reflected in their relationship. The once harmonious couple could no longer live without arguments. The increasing discomfort between them drove my consultee away from home. He had a vibrant social environment. "I realized that marriage is not for me, but I don't want to leave my wife either," he said one day. "I decided to make myself comfortable so that I could continue my marriage. The order I have established outside gives me the strength to bear the heavy responsibility of marriage."

Thus, the fights at home stopped. His wife often went to visit her family. My consultee was also outside at every opportunity. "My wife's trips are good for us," he was saying. "I provide everything she asks for, but no matter what I do, we can't be husband and wife anymore. I began to see her only as the mother of my son. Then my wife decided to go back to work. I also liked that decision, I could be more free now. At that time, I also had an affair. I thought we could end the marriage if my wife got stronger. In a short time, she started to rapidly move up the career ladder, drawing attention due to her appearance and success. This state of hers made me jealous. She was so indifferent to me that I started to think that she had someone else in her life. She surpassed me with her social circle, image, and income. My jealousy towards her and her ignoring me fueled my anger. I used violence against her, albeit I did not mean to. She said she wanted a divorce. It was as if my world collapsed. When I could have left, I didn't, just to take care of her and our son, and I held onto our marriage. As she treated me like this, my growing rage cost me my job, too. I've been unemployed for a year now and my wife gave up on the divorce because she feels sorry for my situation. She treats me like a jerk. I wouldn't stay there for a minute if it wasn't for my son, I'm sure there's nothing left that she hasn't done outside of the house, but what can I do? She's the mother of my child."

Frankly, it was not like many of the marriage stories I often come across. I told him to write down his story. I left the room with a pen and paper in his hand. When I came back he was sobbing. He had begun to see what was going on; the mirror had cleared, and he realized that they had made a trade with his wife, whom he had despised and humiliated. Sometimes we can close our ears to our words while talking to others, but our ears are more sensitive when talking to ourselves. My consultee needed to be alone for a while due to this confrontation he experienced.

The complementary factor in the reunion of this couple was their children. After the child fell into the womb, fateful events began to unfold, and conflict broke out between husband and wife. Both of them tried to maintain the marriage by using the child as an excuse at different times, and the conflict between them grew. In these conflicts, both met with factors that would complement them from the outside. Although this marriage turned into torture for them, they stubbornly kept it going.

After a while, my consultee came to visit me again. His face was alive, his eyes sparkled. He had got a job and started a new life for himself. They stopped persecuting each other after their divorce, and they were happily raising their children in separate homes, like two friends.

They were both happy doing their own thing. They were fed by the appreciation and validation they experienced in this field. Before they got together, they both had successful careers and strong social circles, and once the marital tensions were over, they were happy again in their work and social life because the area where they both felt complete was their careers.

The source of your unhappiness may be the choices you make by the direction of the outside. To end this situation, listen to the voice of your heart, the places where you make calculations may be the areas where you are afraid of being pressured and remove yourself. Courage facilitates you to move forward on your journey to yourself.

Take a look again at the relationships you have had so far: you have invited the other person into your life for which of their qualities to complete you? What you see before you may sometimes be telling you what is missing or in excess.

For a man, his wife or close female reflections represent his material and economic side. His relationship with them also tells about his relationship with money, with the world, and with his own body and health. The way he treats his wife or close female reflections is parallel to his approach to other people and financial matters in life. If a man is deceiving or lying to a woman in any area, it means that he is being deceived somewhere. Whether a man can become or remain wealthy is determined by his relationship with female energy.

For a woman, her husband or close male reflections represent her spiritual side and her relationship with inner inspirations. Her relationship with them tells about the way she is fed from the spiritual realm and her confidence in her insights and inspirations in her decisions about her future. Women who do not listen to their husbands or close male reflections, who talk behind their backs, complain on the inside or outside, look down on them, and who are not sincere in their approach are troubled in their own spiritual world and this is the reason for their inner unrest.

Read Yourself Through Your Behavior

The behaviors and attitudes we exhibit in life are also related to the reflection of what is in our potential.

For instance, those who speak loudly or are shouting hardly listen to themselves and their surroundings. They do not hear at the right time what is said to them, they cannot receive the reminder they need in time. They blame people around them, claiming that what was actually said to them was not said. That information was told to them but while they pretended to listen, they did not because they have closed their ears to themselves and to their heart. Such people may experience kidney and bladder problems. All they need is to be quiet and listen. It will be beneficial to do a speaking fast.

Those who are constantly complaining about any issue say, "They did it, not me, I don't apologize, let them apologize." They cannot back down and have a hard time accepting. They rebel when things do not go their way and they cannot control the outcomes. Because of this approach, they often experience bodily accidents. Gallbladder, bone and stomach problems occur. They can attain the acceptance energy they need by meditating, praying, and getting up before sunrise and listening to their inner voice.

Remember that people are often capable of hiding their true identity, even from themselves. You have probably been wrong about people you thought you had a good idea about. When you ignore the negative aspect of the other person, you turn off your insight. If you witness that a person you find polite is being rude to someone else, and if you continue to ignore it nevertheless, you will be exposed to the same rudeness.

As long as you listen, your insight will always guide you. When you can read what you see, you will read beyond it, too.

Those who feel nervous, shy, and timid when entering unfamiliar environments have been neglected, ignored, or pressured by one of their parents. Therefore, they are used to being under pressure. They feel comfortable in familiar surroundings, shy in unfamiliar places, and are frightened by changes in situations. Because the oppressive parent always told them what to do, they are comfortable in an environment in which they have been taught how to act. They can be the party that has difficulty letting go in relationships; they seek approval from their environment to heal their sense of worthlessness; they may have difficulty changing their point of view. Leaving it to the last minute, they need to be put under pressure to complete a job. Their large intestines, skin, lungs and liver are sensitive. Being free and stepping into the new will give them confidence.

People who are intimidating and prone to physical or verbal aggression at any time basically seek support from people around them. When they find the support they seek, are embraced with love and stop feeling threatened, they would, too, stop threatening others. They tend to have problems with kidneys, ears, bladder, liver, and sexual hormones in the body. It will be very beneficial for them to support organizations that help children, the elderly, and animals.

Those who have memories they want to forget, feel uncomfortable or guilty about will go to extremes about cleanliness and hygiene. The outside is dirty for them, they want to clean it all the time. However, what they truly want to clean is the trace of their experience. They show the same attitude in their personal relationships, they are critical and intrusive. They may especially experience problems with the skin and gallbladder. What they need is to let go of the feeling of having done wrong and accept that life is an experience.

People who accumulate, who have a hard time letting go or spending, and whose frugality turns into stinginess have little confidence in the future. They have a hard time accepting the new because they cannot leave what they have. There are "I know" patterns in their life. Those who are stingy in one area will be wasteful in another. On the contrary, people who spend freely have stinginess in an area where they keep and cannot let go.

Now have a look at your own life! Where are you stingy and where do you spend freely? If there are areas where you give too much, there are areas where you cannot. According to the balance principle of life, wherever you go to extremes, an excess occurs in the opposite direction. If there are areas you spend too much, there are also areas you cannot let go of things.

What You Believe Comes True

It is possible to read what somebody may experience by looking at their beliefs and belief patterns. For example, those who believe that bad things will happen to them when they see a black cat, their beliefs will come true. A consultee of mine told me that his mother and father died at a very young age and that he loved his adoptive family very much. After his second family died, he married at an early age due to the loneliness he felt. His wife, whom he was in love with, left him after a while. Over the years, he was abandoned by his fiancées several times just when he was about to get married. These abandonments started to make him feel insecure about life and he believed that he was not loved.

When I showed him the origin of recurrent events, he saw what kind of belief pattern he had. The things he knew and believed were repeated over and over in his life. That was reality for him.

When he lost his first family, life had embraced him, given him a new family, and his new family, too, lovingly embraced him. He was loved, taken care of, protected, and cared for until he grew up to be an adult. However, in what he had been going through, he focused only on his losses, so his belief pattern became "losing". However, the family that embraced him had raised him with love, protection, and provided him with a good education. He was offered good life opportunities and given confidence instead of the apprehension he gained due to his loss. He himself brought the love and joy of a child to his new family.

Since my consultee could not see his exchange with life, he focused only on losing with a one-sided perspective. He saw himself as someone abandoned, unlovable, and worthless. When he remembered how much he was loved and valued by his adoptive family, the belief that he was loved replaced the feeling of worthlessness caused by the loss he had experienced. Thus, a new era began where he would meet people who knew his worth.

When you look at your experiences from a different angle, you will see that everything you experience stems from your beliefs. When you begin to read the events from your own center, old beliefs are replaced by new understandings. Thus, you will set sail for freedom. Until they find their own path, those who accept to replicate, imitate, and repeat what they see in their family, environment, and life choose to live in the realities of their ancestors.

Move from Seeing Problems to Feeling Responsible

The events and issues that you trouble yourself with are the indicators of the obstacles you put in your way on your journey of evolution. Those who become selfish by saying "I," "me" focus only on their own interests and confine themselves to a narrow area of responsibility. For such people, whatever is in the way of their interest is a problem. That is why, they are always nervous and anxious. The main problem is that they cannot take their own responsibilities and fail to determine their personal space. They get involved in everything, gossip, and become problem-oriented. They have a problem not with the garbage on the floor, but with the one who throws it there. They live a problem-oriented life, not a solution-oriented one.

Solution-oriented people, on the other hand, are focused on making a contribution "for me and for us." "What can I do for me and us?" they ask.

Problem-focused people say, "I'd feel better when you do what I say." As you go from being problem-oriented to being solution-oriented, your responsibilities begin for both yourself and the world you live in. The more a person can take responsibility for himself or herself, the more he or she feels responsible for his/her environment. Therefore, as you know and read yourself, your area of responsibility expands.

We are in a state of being as the fruits of a tree. Even if what is presented to us and what we experience are different, and even if some of us seem to be ahead and some of us behind, we are all in the pursuit of peace.

Opportunities that we seek can be presented to us at any moment, just like a fruit --that has not been able to be fed from the sun until now and remained small because it has been in the back of the garden-- begins to ripen by the rays of the sun reaching it... as long as we demand to embrace and receive, and be ready for it.

When you are drowning in problems, cannot find the answers to your questions and think you are lost, open your compass and be sure to be embraced. When you stop worshipping the light and avoid turning into darkness, when you accept what is by not being on either side of giving and receiving but being present in both, you will be at peace with the guidance of your heart. You have the potential to stray into darkness as much as worshipping the light. You are in balance when you can embrace both.

You are in heaven the moment you are at peace and in the One's presence, and meet the one reflected in the mirror.

Notes:

....

....

....

....

....

....

....

....

....

....

....

....

....

....